Everything the Bible Says About Money

EVERYTHING
the Bible Says About
MONEY

BETHANY HOUSE PUBLISHERS
a division of Baker Publishing Group
Minneapolis, Minnesota

Compiled by Lin Johnson
Series editors: Kyle Duncan and Andy McGuire

Published by Bethany House Publishers
11400 Hampshire Avenue South
Bloomington, Minnesota 55438
www.bethanyhouse.com

Bethany House Publishers is a division of
Baker Publishing Group, Grand Rapids, Michigan

Printed in the United States of America

Library of Congress Cataloging-in-Publication Data
Everything the Bible says about money / [compiled by Lin Johnson]
    p. cm.
    Includes bibliographical references.
    Summary: "A gathering of all the Bible's references to money, including verses on spending, saving, earning, tithing, lending, wealth, and poverty. Also provides very brief context and commentary"—Provided by publisher.
    ISBN 978-0-7642-0909-3 (pbk. : alk. paper)
    1. Money—Biblical teaching. 2. Bible—Quotations. 3. Money—Quotations, maxims, etc.
I. Johnson, Lin.
BS680.M57E94 2011
220.8'3324—dc23   2011026705

Cover design by Eric Walljasper

11 12 13 14 15 16 17   7 6 5 4 3 2 1

CONTENTS

Contents

INTRODUCTION

How much time did you spend over the last month earning and investing money, buying what you needed and some of what you wanted, paying your bills, and wishing you had a little more left over afterward? If you're like most people, money and issues surrounding it consume a lot of your thoughts and time.

Money is such an important subject that publishing houses produce many books about it every year. In fact, Amazon.com lists almost 94,000 books on the topic. Magazines and newsletters like *Money, Smart Money, Consumer Reports Money Advisor,* and *Christian Money Management* strive to help subscribers get more money and use it wisely. That's a lot of words devoted to the topic!

But what does God have to say about money? The Bible addresses the issue a lot, since how you deal with your money is an indication of what's in your heart, which God cares very much about. His perspective on money often differs from the views our culture and media bombard us with.

Although written centuries ago, Agur's prayer in Proverbs 30:8–9 (ESV) provides a model for us to pray today: "Remove far from me falsehood and lying; give me neither poverty nor riches; feed me with the food that is needful for me, lest I be full and deny you and say, 'Who is the LORD?' or lest I be poor and steal and profane the name of my God."

By showing you what the Bible says about money, this book will help you gain Agur's—and God's—perspective.

IT'S NOT YOURS

Your bank accounts have your name on them. Your pay-
checks are made out to you. You spend time—probably
more than you want to—obsessing over your finances: whether
you have enough money to pay your bills, if you can afford
to buy what you want, if you can afford to retire someday.

Even though you may view your money as yours, it's not.
The Bible teaches that everything we have, including money,
is from God. Recognizing that fact can free you from anxiety
over your finances because God will provide enough. He
will use your ability to earn money, sometimes in ways you
can't imagine.

Your Money Comes From God

As Moses reminded the Israelites, But remember the LORD your God, for it is he who gives you the ability to produce wealth, and so confirms his covenant, which he swore to your ancestors, as it is today. **(DEUTERONOMY 8:18 NIV)**

⸻

Blessed are You, O LORD God of Israel our father, forever and ever.

Yours, O LORD, is the greatness and the power and the glory and the victory and the majesty, indeed everything that is in the heavens and the earth; Yours is the dominion, O LORD, and You exalt Yourself as head over all.

Both riches and honor come from You, and You rule over all, and in Your hand is power and might; and it lies in Your hand to make great and to strengthen everyone.

Now therefore, our God, we thank You, and praise Your glorious name.

But who am I and who are my people that we should be able to offer as generously as this? For all things come from You, and from Your hand we have given You.

For we are sojourners before You, and tenants, as all our fathers were; our days on the earth are like a shadow, and there is no hope.

O LORD our God, all this abundance that we have provided to build You a house for Your holy name, it is from Your hand, and all is Yours. **(1 CHRONICLES 29:10–16 NASB)**

This is King David's prayer as he and the Israelites prepared to build the Temple for worshiping God.

⸻

The earth is the Lord's, and all its fullness, the world and those who dwell therein. **(PSALM 24:1 NKJV)**

⸎

For every beast of the forest is Mine, and the cattle on a thousand hills. **(PSALM 50:10 NKJV)**

⸎

And it is a good thing to receive wealth from God and the good health to enjoy it. To enjoy your work and accept your lot in life—this is indeed a gift from God. **(ECCLESIASTES 5:19 NLT)**

⸎

The silver is mine, and the gold is mine, saith the Lord of hosts. **(HAGGAI 2:8 KJV)**

⸎

For everything comes from him [God] and exists by his power and is intended for his glory. All glory to him forever! Amen. **(ROMANS 11:36 NLT)**

God Gives His Children Enough

The Lord is my shepherd; I have all that I need. **(PSALM 23:1 NLT)**

⸎

I was young and now I am old, yet I have never seen the righteous forsaken or their children begging bread. **(PSALM 37:25 NIV)**

⸎

But my God shall supply all your need according to his riches in glory by Christ Jesus. **(PHILIPPIANS 4:19 KJV)**

Choose Money or God

And keep the charge of the LORD your God, walking in his ways and keeping his statutes, his commandments, his rules, and his testimonies, as it is written in the Law of Moses, that you may prosper in all that you do and wherever you turn. (**1 KINGS 2:3** ESV)

As King David was dying, he told his son Solomon to put God first; then he would be prosperous.

Submit to God and be at peace with him; in this way prosperity will come to you. (**JOB 22:21** NIV)

Don't make your living by extortion or put your hope in stealing. And if your wealth increases, don't make it the center of your life. (**PSALM 62:10** NLT)

Choose my instruction rather than silver, and knowledge rather than pure gold. For wisdom is far more valuable than rubies. Nothing you desire can compare with it. (**PROVERBS 8:10–11** NLT)

Riches and honor are with me, Enduring wealth and righteousness.

My fruit is better than gold, even pure gold, and my yield better than choicest silver.

I walk in the way of righteousness, in the midst of the paths of justice, to endow those who love me with wealth, that I may fill their treasuries. (**PROVERBS 8:18–21** NASB)

A thick bankroll is no help when life falls apart, but a principled life can stand up to the worst. **(PROVERBS 11:4** THE MESSAGE**)**

He who trusts in his riches will fall, but the righteous will flourish like foliage. **(PROVERBS 11:28** NKJV**)**

Get wisdom—it's worth more than money; choose insight over income every time. **(PROVERBS 16:16** THE MESSAGE**)**

In Gibeon the Lord appeared to Solomon in a dream at night. He said, "What can I give you?"

Solomon responded, "You've shown great love to my father David, who was your servant. He lived in your presence with truth, righteousness, and commitment. And you continued to show him your great love by giving him a son to sit on his throne today.

"Lord my God, although I'm young and inexperienced, you've made me king in place of my father David. I'm among your people whom you have chosen. They are too numerous to count or record. Give me a heart that listens so that I can judge your people and tell the difference between good and evil. After all, who can judge this great people of yours?"

The Lord was pleased that Solomon asked for this. God replied, "You've asked for this and not for a long life, or riches for yourself, or the death of your enemies. Instead, you've asked for understanding so that you can do what is right. So I'm going to do what you've asked. I'm giving you a wise and understanding heart so that there will never be anyone like you. I'm also giving you what you haven't asked for—riches and honor—so that no other king will be like you as long as you live. And if you follow me and obey my laws and commands as your father David did, then I will also give you a long life" (1 KINGS 3:5–14 GOD'S WORD).

When God asked Solomon what he wanted, he asked for wisdom, not riches. But God blessed him with both wisdom and riches. In the next passage we see how God made him wealthy beyond comprehension.

The gold that came to Solomon in one year weighed 49,950 pounds, not counting the gold which came from the merchants, the traders' profits, all the Arab kings, and the governors of the country.

King Solomon made 200 large shields of hammered gold, using 15 pounds of gold on each shield. He also made 300 small shields of hammered gold, using four pounds of gold on each shield. The king put them in the hall which he called the Forest of Lebanon.

The king also made a large ivory throne and covered it with fine gold. Six steps led to the throne. Carved into the back of the throne was a calf's head. There were armrests on both sides of the seat. Two lions stood beside the armrests. Twelve lions stood on six steps, one on each side. Nothing like this had been made for any other kingdom.

All King Solomon's cups were gold, and all the utensils for the hall which he called the Forest of Lebanon were fine gold. (Nothing was silver, because it wasn't considered valuable in Solomon's time.) The king had a fleet headed for Tarshish with Hiram's fleet. Once every three years the Tarshish fleet would bring gold, silver, ivory, apes, and monkeys.

In wealth and wisdom King Solomon was greater than all the other kings of the world. The whole world wanted to listen to the wisdom that God gave Solomon. So everyone who came brought him gifts: articles of silver and gold, clothing, weapons, spices, horses, and mules. This happened year after year. (1 KINGS 10:14–25 GOD'S WORD)

Whoever loves money never has enough; whoever loves wealth is never satisfied with their income. This too is meaningless. As goods increase, so do those who consume them. And what benefit are they to the owners except to feast their eyes on them? (ECCLESIASTES 5:10–11 NIV)

Ecclesiastes was written by Solomon. If anyone knew about wealth, it was him.

Why do you brag about your valleys, your fertile valleys, you unfaithful people? You trust your treasures. You think, "Who would attack me?" I am going to bring terror on you from all around, declares the Almighty Lord of Armies. Everyone will be scattered. No one will gather the refugees. (JEREMIAH 49:4–5 GOD'S WORD)

Jesus warned: Don't store up treasures here on earth, where moths eat them and rust destroys them, and where thieves break in and steal. Store your treasures in heaven, where moths and rust cannot destroy, and thieves do not break in and steal. Wherever your treasure is, there the desires of your heart will also be. . . .

No one can serve two masters. For you will hate one and love the other; you will be devoted to one and despise the other. You cannot serve both God and money. **(MATTHEW 6:19–21, 24** NLT**)**

Jesus asked his disciples, For what will it profit a man if he gains the whole world and forfeits his soul? Or what will a man give in exchange for his soul? **(MATTHEW 16:26** NASB**)**

Then the Pharisees went out and laid plans to trap him in his words. They sent their disciples to him along with the Herodians. "Teacher," they said, "we know you are a man of integrity and that you teach the way of God in accordance with the truth. You aren't swayed by others, because you pay no attention to who they are. Tell us then, what is your opinion? Is it right to pay taxes to Caesar or not?"

But Jesus, knowing their evil intent, said, "You hypocrites, why are you trying to trap me? Show me the coin used for paying the tax." They brought him a denarius, and he asked them, "Whose image is this? And whose inscription?"

"Caesar's," they replied.

Then he said to them, "Give back to Caesar what is Caesar's, and to God what is God's."

When they heard this, they were amazed. So they left him and went away. **(MATTHEW 22:15–22** NIV**)**

What was Jesus saying to the Pharisees, and, ultimately, to us? According to commentaries, there are two lessons we can learn. First, we should obey the law and not cheat the government out of the money we owe. Second, and more important, we should give to God what is owed to him, which is everything: our money, our time, our love, our worship, etc.

◆◆————◆◆

Then Jesus, looking at him, loved him, and said to him, "One thing you lack: Go your way, sell whatever you have and give to the poor, and you will have treasure in heaven; and come, take up the cross, and follow Me."

But he was sad at this word, and went away sorrowful, for he had great possessions.

Then Jesus looked around and said to His disciples, "How hard it is for those who have riches to enter the kingdom of God!" And the disciples were astonished at His words. But Jesus answered again and said to them, "Children, how hard it is for those who trust in riches to enter the kingdom of God! It is easier for a camel to go through the eye of a needle than for a rich man to enter the kingdom of God."

And they were greatly astonished, saying among themselves, "Who then can be saved?" **(MARK 10:21–26 NKJV).**

This rich young ruler loved his money too much to give it up in order to put his faith in God.

◆◆————◆◆

"Yes, a person is a fool to store up earthly wealth but not have a rich relationship with God."

Then, turning to his disciples, Jesus said, "That is why I tell you not to worry about everyday life—whether you have enough food to eat or enough clothes to wear. For life is more than food, and your body more than clothing. Look at the ravens. They don't plant or harvest or store food in barns, for

God feeds them. And you are far more valuable to him than any birds! Can all your worries add a single moment to your life? And if worry can't accomplish a little thing like that, what's the use of worrying over bigger things?

"Look at the lilies and how they grow. They don't work or make their clothing, yet Solomon in all his glory was not dressed as beautifully as they are. And if God cares so wonderfully for flowers that are here today and thrown into the fire tomorrow, he will certainly care for you. Why do you have so little faith?

"And don't be concerned about what to eat and what to drink. Don't worry about such things. These things dominate the thoughts of unbelievers all over the world, but your Father already knows your needs. Seek the Kingdom of God above all else, and he will give you everything you need.

"So don't be afraid, little flock. For it gives your Father great happiness to give you the Kingdom.

"Sell your possessions and give to those in need. This will store up treasure for you in heaven! And the purses of heaven never get old or develop holes. Your treasure will be safe; no thief can steal it and no moth can destroy it. Wherever your treasure is, there the desires of your heart will also be" **(LUKE 12:21–34 NLT).**

Here Jesus taught that you don't need to worry about the things money buys, since God already knows what you need and will take care of you. It's more important to store up spiritual treasures than to accumulate a lot of money.

But Peter said to him, "May your silver perish with you, because you thought you could obtain the gift of God with money!" **(ACTS 8:20 NASB).**

Peter rebuked Simon the magician for trying to buy the authority to give the Holy Spirit to people who believed in Jesus as Savior from sin.

For the love of money is a root of all kinds of evils. It is through this craving that some have wandered away from the faith and pierced themselves with many pangs. **(1 TIMOTHY 6:10 ESV)**

Paul wrote these words in a letter to Timothy.

But know this, that in the last days perilous times will come: For men will be lovers of themselves, lovers of money, boasters, proud, blasphemers, disobedient to parents, unthankful, unholy. **(2 TIMOTHY 3:1–2 NKJV)**

God Is in Control

While [Elisha] was still talking to them, the messenger arrived. He said to Elisha, "This severe famine is from the LORD. Why should I wait any longer for the LORD to help us?"

Elisha answered, "Listen to the word of the LORD! This is what the LORD says: About this time tomorrow 24 cups of the best flour will sell for half an ounce of silver in the gateway to Samaria. And 48 cups of barley will sell for half an ounce of silver."

The servant on whose arm the king was leaning answered the man of God, "Could this happen even if the LORD poured rain through windows in the sky?"

Elisha replied, "You will see it with your own eyes, but you won't eat any of it."

Four men with skin diseases were at the entrance of the city gate. One of them asked, "Why are we sitting here waiting to die? If we go into the city, the famine is also there, and we'll still die. But if we stay here, we'll die. So let's go to the Aramean camp. If they give us something to keep us alive, we'll live. But if they kill us, we'll die anyway." So they started out at dusk to go into the Aramean camp. When they came to the edge of the camp, no one was there.

(The LORD had made the Aramean army hear what sounded like chariots, horses, and a large army. The Aramean soldiers said to one another, "The king of Israel has hired the Hittite and Egyptian kings to attack us!" So at dusk they fled. They abandoned the camp as it was with its tents, horses, and donkeys and ran for their lives.)

When the men with skin diseases came to the edge of the camp, they went into a tent, ate and drank, and carried off the silver, gold, and clothes they found in that tent. They went away and hid them. Then they came back, went into another tent, carried off its contents, went away, and hid them.

Then they said to one another, "What we're doing is not right. This is a day of good news, and we're not telling anyone about it. If we wait until morning when it's light out, we'll be punished. Let's bring the news to the royal palace." So they called the city gatekeepers and told them, "We went into the Aramean camp, and we didn't see or hear anyone. The horses and donkeys were still tied up. Even the tents were left exactly as they were."

The gatekeepers announced the news to the royal palace. So the king got up at night and told his officers what the Arameans had planned for them. He said, "They know we're starving, so they've left the camp to hide in the countryside. They're thinking, 'When they've left the city, we'll capture them alive and get into the city.'"

One of his officers replied, "Please let some men take five of the horses that are left here. Those men will be no worse off than the rest of the Israelites who are dying. Let's send them to take a look." So they took two chariots with horses, and the king sent them to follow the Aramean army and told them to find out what happened. They followed them as far as the Jordan River and saw how the whole road was littered with clothes and equipment that the Arameans had thrown away in their hurry. The messengers returned and told the king about it.

So the people went out and looted the Aramean camp. Then 24 cups of the best flour sold for half an ounce of silver, and 48 cups of barley sold for half an ounce of silver, as the LORD had predicted.

The king appointed the servant on whose arm he used to lean to be in charge of the gate. But the people trampled him to death in the gateway, as the man of God had predicted when the king came to him. (It happened exactly as the man of God told the king, "Forty-eight cups of barley will sell for half an ounce of silver. And twenty-four cups of the best flour will sell for half an ounce of silver. This will happen about this time tomorrow in the gateway to Samaria." Then the servant answered the man of God, "Could this happen even if the LORD poured rain through windows in the sky?" Elisha answered, "You will see it with your own eyes, but you won't eat any of it.") So this is what happened to the king's servant: The people trampled him to death in the gateway. (2 KINGS 6:33–7:20 GOD'S WORD)

There are many lessons within this story, but one important one is that God knows what will happen and is in control of everything, including the economy. Prices, jobs, famine, etc., are no match for the Lord.

Now listen, you who say, "Today or tomorrow we will go to this or that city, spend a year there, carry on business and make money." Why, you do not even know what will happen tomorrow. What is your life? You are a mist that appears for a little while and then vanishes. Instead, you ought to say, "If it is the Lord's will, we will live and do this or that." As it is, you boast in your arrogant schemes. All such boasting is evil. **(JAMES 4:13–16 NIV)**

Presuming you'll have even one more day to live and make money is putting God second.

MAKING MONEY

Few people are born with fortunes large enough that they don't need to earn a living. Perhaps you've wished you were a trust-fund baby or are convinced you were born to be rich and lead a life of leisure, but your parents didn't get the memo.

Work is the most common way to make money, whether you view your job as something to look forward to, a necessary evil to pay the bills, or something to dread five days a week. Regardless, some people look for ways to get money by other means, such as get-rich-quick schemes.

Sure, God could supernaturally provide everything you need, including a fat bank account, and sometimes he does give you money in unexpected ways. But most of your money will probably come from working.

So what does the Bible say about earning money and—from the other side—paying wages?

Earning Income

After Jacob had stayed with him for a whole month, Laban said to him, "Just because you are a relative of mine, should you work for me for nothing? Tell me what your wages should be" **(GENESIS 29:14–15 NIV).**

Laban was Jacob's uncle. He understood that a worker, even a relative, deserves to earn an income.

Don't make your living by extortion or put your hope in stealing. And if your wealth increases, don't make it the center of your life. **(PSALM 62:10 NLT)**

Ill-gotten treasures have no lasting value, but righteousness delivers from death. **(PROVERBS 10:2 NIV)**

Idle hands make one poor, but diligent hands bring riches. **(PROVERBS 10:4 HCSB)**

A wicked person earns deceptive wages, but the one who sows righteousness reaps a sure reward. **(PROVERBS 11:18 NIV)**

Honest work pays off.

Those who work their land will have abundant food, but those who chase fantasies have no sense. **(PROVERBS 12:11 NIV)**

Lazy people want much but get little, but those who work hard will prosper. **(PROVERBS 13:4 NLT)**

In all labor there is profit, but idle chatter leads only to poverty. **(PROVERBS 14:23 NKJV)**

The person who labors, labors for himself, For his hungry mouth drives him on. **(PROVERBS 16:26 NKJV)**

Wealth created by a lying tongue is a vanishing mist and a deadly trap. **(PROVERBS 21:6 NLT)**

Lazy people's desire for sleep will kill them, because they refuse to work. All day long they wish for more, but good people give without holding back. **(PROVERBS 21:25–26 NCV)**

Don't wear yourself out trying to get rich. Be wise enough to know when to quit. **(PROVERBS 23:4 NLT)**

Those who work their land will have abundant food, but those who chase fantasies will have their fill of poverty. **(PROVERBS 28:19 NIV)**

There is nothing better for a man than to eat and drink and tell himself that his labor is good. This also I have seen that it is from the hand of God. (ECCLESIASTES 2:24 NASB)

I know that there is nothing better for them than to rejoice and to do good in one's lifetime; moreover, that every man who eats and drinks sees good in all his labor—it is the gift of God. (ECCLESIASTES 3:12–13 NASB)

What shall I say about the homes of the wicked filled with treasures gained by cheating? What about the disgusting practice of measuring out grain with dishonest measures? How can I tolerate your merchants who use dishonest scales and weights? The rich among you have become wealthy through extortion and violence. Your citizens are so used to lying that their tongues can no longer tell the truth.

Therefore, I will wound you! I will bring you to ruin for all your sins. You will eat but never have enough. Your hunger pangs and emptiness will remain. And though you try to save your money, it will come to nothing in the end. You will save a little, but I will give it to those who conquer you. (MICAH 6:10–14 NLT)

Through the Old Testament prophet Micah, God rebuked his people for not working honestly to get their money.

For the kingdom of heaven is like a landowner who went out early in the morning to hire workers for his vineyard.

He agreed to pay them a denarius for the day and sent them into his vineyard.

About nine in the morning he went out and saw others standing in the marketplace doing nothing. He told them, "You also go and work in my vineyard, and I will pay you whatever is right." So they went.

He went out again about noon and about three in the afternoon and did the same thing. About five in the afternoon he went out and found still others standing around. He asked them, "Why have you been standing here all day long doing nothing?"

"Because no one has hired us," they answered.

He said to them, "You also go and work in my vineyard."

When evening came, the owner of the vineyard said to his foreman, "Call the workers and pay them their wages, beginning with the last ones hired and going on to the first."

The workers who were hired about five in the afternoon came and each received a denarius. So when those came who were hired first, they expected to receive more. But each one of them also received a denarius. When they received it, they began to grumble against the landowner. "These who were hired last worked only one hour," they said, "and you have made them equal to us who have borne the burden of the work and the heat of the day."

But he answered one of them, "I am not being unfair to you, friend. Didn't you agree to work for a denarius? Take your pay and go. I want to give the one who was hired last the same as I gave you. Don't I have the right to do what I want with my own money? Or are you envious because I am generous?"

So the last will be first, and the first will be last. **(MATTHEW 20:1–16 NIV)**

Although money wasn't the main point of this story Jesus told, he does teach that workers who agree to a certain wage have no cause to be jealous of others who get paid more.

Paul wrote to several churches about working hard to earn money:

Let him who stole steal no longer, but rather let him labor, working with his hands what is good, that he may have something to give him who has need. (EPHESIANS 4:28 NKJV)

Whatever you do, work heartily, as for the Lord and not for men, knowing that from the Lord you will receive the inheritance as your reward. You are serving the Lord Christ. (COLOSSIANS 3:23–24 ESV)

Make it your goal to live a quiet life, minding your own business and working with your hands, just as we instructed you before. Then people who are not Christians will respect the way you live, and you will not need to depend on others. (1 THESSALONIANS 4:11–12 NLT)

And now, dear brothers and sisters, we give you this command in the name of our Lord Jesus Christ: Stay away from all believers who live idle lives and don't follow the tradition they received from us. For you know that you ought to imitate us. We were not idle when we were with you. We never accepted food from anyone without paying for it. We worked hard day and night so we would not be a burden to any of you. We certainly had the right to ask you to feed us, but we wanted to give you an example to follow. Even while we were with you, we gave you this command: "Those unwilling to work will not get to eat."

Yet we hear that some of you are living idle lives, refusing to work and meddling in other people's business. We command such people and urge them in the name of the Lord Jesus Christ to settle down and work to earn their own living. **(2 THESSALONIANS 3:6–12 NLT)**

Get-Rich-Quick Schemes

Wealth from get-rich-quick schemes quickly disappears; wealth from hard work grows over time. **(PROVERBS 13:11 NLT)**

Good planning and hard work lead to prosperity, but hasty shortcuts lead to poverty. **(PROVERBS 21:5 NLT)**

A miser in a hurry to get rich doesn't know that he'll end up broke. **(PROVERBS 28:22 THE MESSAGE)**

Paying Wages

Do not defraud or rob your neighbor. Do not hold back the wages of a hired worker overnight. **(LEVITICUS 19:13 NIV)**

In Moses' time, workers were paid daily, so it was a hardship for them to have to wait for the money they earned. Today, it would be a matter of paying regularly: weekly, biweekly, or monthly.

Do not take advantage of a hired worker who is poor and needy, whether that worker is a fellow Israelite or a foreigner residing in one of your towns. Pay them their wages each day before sunset, because they are poor and are counting on it. Otherwise they may cry to the LORD against you, and you will be guilty of sin. **(DEUTERONOMY 24:14–15 NIV)**

"So I will come to put you on trial. I will be quick to testify against sorcerers, adulterers and perjurers, against those who defraud laborers of their wages, who oppress the widows and the fatherless, and deprive the foreigners among you of justice, but do not fear me," says the LORD Almighty. **(MALACHI 3:5 NIV)**

God will punish employers who don't pay the people who work for them.
According to Jesus,

The worker deserves his wages. **(LUKE 10:7 NIV)**

Now to the one who works, wages are not credited as a gift but as an obligation. **(ROMANS 4:4 NIV)**

We hear that some among you are idle and disruptive. They are not busy; they are busybodies. Such people we command and urge in the Lord Jesus Christ to settle down and earn the food they eat. **(2 THESSALONIANS 3:11–12 NIV)**

The elders who direct the affairs of the church well are worthy of double honor, especially those whose work is preaching and teaching. For Scripture says, "Do not muzzle an ox while it is treading out the grain," and "The worker deserves his wages" **(1 TIMOTHY 5:17–18 NIV).**

Like animals that were entitled to eat grain while threshing it ("Do not muzzle an ox"), workers today are entitled to fair wages.

Look! The wages you failed to pay the workers who mowed your fields are crying out against you. The cries of the harvesters have reached the ears of the Lord Almighty. **(JAMES 5:4 NIV)**

Paying Taxes

There have been mighty kings also over Jerusalem, which have ruled over all countries beyond the river; and toll, tribute, and custom, was paid unto them. **(EZRA 4:20 KJV)**

Even in Old Testament times, people paid taxes to governing bodies.

When [Jesus' disciples] had come to Capernaum, those who received the temple tax came to Peter and said, "Does your Teacher not pay the temple tax?"

He said, "Yes."

And when he had come into the house, Jesus anticipated him, saying, "What do you think, Simon? From whom do the kings of the earth take customs or taxes, from their sons or from strangers?"

Peter said to Him, "From strangers."

Jesus said to him, "Then the sons are free. Nevertheless, lest we offend them, go to the sea, cast in a hook, and take the fish that comes up first. And when you have opened its mouth, you will find a piece of money; take that and give it to them for Me and you" (MATTHEW 17:24–27 NKJV).

Keeping a close watch on him, [the religious leaders] sent spies, who pretended to be sincere. They hoped to catch Jesus in something he said, so that they might hand him over to the power and authority of the governor. So the spies questioned him: "Teacher, we know that you speak and teach what is right, and that you do not show partiality but teach the way of God in accordance with the truth. Is it right for us to pay taxes to Caesar or not?"

He saw through their duplicity and said to them, "Show me a denarius. Whose image and inscription are on it?"

"Caesar's," they replied.

He said to them, "Then give back to Caesar what is Caesar's, and to God what is God's" (LUKE 20:20–25 NIV).

Let every person be subject to the governing authorities. For there is no authority except from God, and those that exist have been instituted by God. Therefore whoever resists the authorities resists what God has appointed, and those who resist will incur judgment. For rulers are not a terror to good conduct, but to bad. Would you have no fear of the one who is in authority? Then do what is good, and you will receive his approval, for he is God's servant for your good. But if you do wrong, be afraid, for he does not bear the sword in vain. For he is the servant of God, an avenger who carries out God's wrath on the wrongdoer. Therefore one must be in subjection, not only to avoid God's wrath but also for the sake of conscience. For because of this you also pay taxes, for the authorities are ministers of God, attending to this very thing.

Pay to all what is owed to them: taxes to whom taxes are owed, revenue to whom revenue is owed, respect to whom respect is owed, honor to whom honor is owed. **(ROMANS 13:1–7** ESV**)**

Submit to every human institution because of the Lord, whether to the Emperor as the supreme authority, or to governors as those sent out by him to punish those who do evil and to praise those who do good. **(1 PETER 2:13–14** HCSB**)**

Submitting to governments includes obeying the laws about paying taxes.

CONTENT WITH WHAT YOU HAVE

Television and radio commercials, magazine and newspaper ads, billboards, and what other people own all entice us to buy more.

Within months, or often weeks, the computer or cell phone you bought will be outdated, and you'll be tempted to trade it for a faster, newer model with more features.

Perhaps your closets and drawers burst with stuff you've bought and may not use anymore. Or your basement and attic are so full you can't store another box there, and you're considering renting a self-storage unit for the overflow—if you haven't already.

Are you feeling like what you have isn't enough?

Contentment doesn't come easy, but the Bible teaches it's possible to be content with what you have.

Better is the little of the righteous than the abundance of many wicked. **(PSALM 37:16 NASB)**

Better is a little with righteousness than great revenues without right. **(PROVERBS 16:8 KJV)**

Remove far from me falsehood and lying; give me neither poverty nor riches; feed me with the food that is needful for me, lest I be full and deny you and say, "Who is the Lord?" or lest I be poor and steal and profane the name of my God. **(PROVERBS 30:8–9 ESV)**

Give us this day our daily bread. **(MATTHEW 6:11 KJV)**

Jesus taught us how to pray. Rather than worrying, ask God daily for what you need.

Then I observed that most people are motivated to success because they envy their neighbors. But this, too, is meaningless—like chasing the wind. **(ECCLESIASTES 4:4 NLT)**

There was a man all alone; he had neither son nor brother. There was no end to his toil, yet his eyes were not content with his wealth.

"For whom am I toiling," he asked, "and why am I depriving myself of enjoyment?"

This too is meaningless—a miserable business!
(ECCLESIASTES 4:8 NIV)

People who work hard sleep well, whether they eat little or much. But the rich seldom get a good night's sleep.
(ECCLESIASTES 5:12 NLT)

Enjoy what you have rather than desiring what you don't have. Just dreaming about nice things is meaningless—like chasing the wind. **(ECCLESIASTES 6:9 NLT)**

Jesus taught, That is why I tell you not to worry about everyday life—whether you have enough food and drink, or enough clothes to wear. Isn't life more than food, and your body more than clothing? Look at the birds. They don't plant or harvest or store food in barns, for your heavenly Father feeds them. And aren't you far more valuable to him than they are? Can all your worries add a single moment to your life?

And why worry about your clothing? Look at the lilies of the field and how they grow. They don't work or make their clothing, yet Solomon in all his glory was not dressed as beautifully as they are. And if God cares so wonderfully for wildflowers that are here today and thrown into the fire tomorrow, he will certainly care for you. Why do you have so little faith?

So don't worry about these things, saying, "What will we eat? What will we drink? What will we wear?" These things dominate the thoughts of unbelievers, but your heavenly Father already knows all your needs. Seek the Kingdom of God above all else, and live righteously, and he will give you everything you need.

So don't worry about tomorrow, for tomorrow will bring its own worries. Today's trouble is enough for today. (MATTHEW 6:25–34 NLT)

> *Because God will take care of your needs, you can be content with what he's given you.*

"What should we do?" asked some soldiers.

John replied, "Don't extort money or make false accusations. And be content with your pay" (LUKE 3:14 NLT).

Our hearts ache, but we always have joy. We are poor, but we give spiritual riches to others. We own nothing, and yet we have everything. (2 CORINTHIANS 6:10 NLT)

Paul wrote to the church at Ephesus, I rejoiced greatly in the Lord that at last you renewed your concern for me. Indeed, you were concerned, but you had no opportunity to show it. I am not saying this because I am in need, for I have learned to be content whatever the circumstances. I know what it is to be in need, and I know what it is to have plenty. I have learned the secret of being content in any and every situation, whether well fed or hungry, whether living in plenty or in want. I can do all this through him who gives me strength. (PHILIPPIANS 4:10–13 NIV)

Paul later wrote to Timothy, Now there is great gain in godliness with contentment, for we brought nothing into the world, and we cannot take anything out of the world. But if we have food and clothing, with these we will be content. **(1 TIMOTHY 6:6–8** ESV**)**

Keep your lives free from the love of money and be content with what you have, because God has said, "Never will I leave you; never will I forsake you" **(HEBREWS 13:5** NIV**).**

USING YOUR MONEY WISELY

Do these scenarios sound familiar?

Although you may earn a good salary, you have little money left after paying bills to save for unexpected repairs, replacing expensive items, or taking a much-needed vacation.

Perhaps you've been looking at your savings account and realize that if you lose your job, you don't have enough of a financial cushion to pay your bills for a few months until you find another job.

Or you're thinking ahead to retirement, but with little money set aside to live on, you may not be able to afford to retire when you want to—or ever.

Not only does the Bible offer guidance about earning money, but also about how to use your money wisely.

Saving

Take a lesson from the ants, you lazybones. Learn from their ways and become wise! Though they have no prince or governor or ruler to make them work, they labor hard all summer, gathering food for the winter. **(PROVERBS 6:6–8 NLT)**

Good planning and hard work lead to prosperity, but hasty shortcuts lead to poverty. **(PROVERBS 21:5 NLT)**

It's better to plan ahead and save money for what you want than to spend money you don't have to get it now.

The wise have wealth and luxury, but fools spend whatever they get. **(PROVERBS 21:20 NLT)**

A prudent person foresees danger and takes precautions. The simpleton goes blindly on and suffers the consequences. **(PROVERBS 22:3; 27:12 NLT)**

This verse is repeated twice in Proverbs. Preparing financially for future needs by saving money will prevent money problems later.

Spending

He who is faithful in a very little thing is faithful also in much; and he who is unrighteous in a very little thing is unrighteous also in much.

Therefore if you have not been faithful in the use of unrighteous wealth, who will entrust the true riches to you?

And if you have not been faithful in the use of that which is another's, who will give you that which is your own?

No servant can serve two masters; for either he will hate the one and love the other, or else he will be devoted to one and despise the other. You cannot serve God and wealth. (LUKE 16:10–13 NASB)

God expects people to use their money wisely and to be faithful with what they have, no matter how little it is.

In this case, moreover, it is required of stewards that one be found trustworthy. (1 CORINTHIANS 4:2 NASB)

A steward is a person who is put in charge of someone else's money and/or possessions. God trusts you with the money you have and expects you to use it wisely, not spending it carelessly or wasting it.

Now I am ready to visit you for the third time, and I will not be a burden to you, because what I want is not your possessions but you. After all, children should not have to save up for their parents, but parents for their children. (2 CORINTHIANS 12:14 NIV)

Take care of widows who are destitute. If a widow has family members to take care of her, let them learn that religion begins at their own doorstep and that they should pay back with gratitude some of what they have received. This pleases God immensely. You can tell a legitimate widow by the way she has put all her hope in God, praying to him constantly for the needs of others as well as her own. But a widow who exploits people's emotions and pocketbooks—well, there's nothing to her. Tell these things to the people so that they will do the right thing in their extended family. Anyone who neglects to care for family members in need repudiates the faith. That's worse than refusing to believe in the first place. (1 TIMOTHY 5:4–8 THE MESSAGE)

Investing

The house of the righteous contains great treasure, but the income of the wicked brings ruin. (PROVERBS 15:6 NIV)

One interpretation of this verse is that godly people who invest their money wisely will not become broke. Another interpretation is that this is a reminder to wicked people that God will cause them to lose money they got in dishonest ways.

There is a grievous evil which I have seen under the sun: riches being hoarded by their owner to his hurt. When those riches were lost through a bad investment and he had fathered a son, then there was nothing to support him. (ECCLESIASTES 5:13–14 NASB)

Again, [the kingdom of heaven] will be like a man going on a journey, who called his servants and entrusted his wealth to them. To one he gave five bags of gold, to another two bags, and to another one bag, each according to his ability. Then he went on his journey. The man who had received five bags of gold went at once and put his money to work and gained five bags more. So also, the one with two bags of gold gained two more. But the man who had received one bag went off, dug a hole in the ground and hid his master's money.

After a long time the master of those servants returned and settled accounts with them. The man who had received five bags of gold brought the other five. "Master," he said, "you entrusted me with five bags of gold. See, I have gained five more."

His master replied, "Well done, good and faithful servant! You have been faithful with a few things; I will put you in charge of many things. Come and share your master's happiness!"

The man with two bags of gold also came. "Master," he said, "you entrusted me with two bags of gold; see, I have gained two more."

His master replied, "Well done, good and faithful servant! You have been faithful with a few things; I will put you in charge of many things. Come and share your master's happiness!"

Then the man who had received one bag of gold came. "Master," he said, "I knew that you are a hard man, harvesting where you have not sown and gathering where you have not scattered seed. So I was afraid and went out and hid your gold in the ground. See, here is what belongs to you."

His master replied, "You wicked, lazy servant! So you knew that I harvest where I have not sown and gather where I have not scattered seed? Well then, you should have put my money on deposit with the bankers, so that when I returned I would have received it back with interest.

"So take the bag of gold from him and give it to the one who has ten bags. For whoever has will be given more, and they will have an abundance. Whoever does not have, even what they have will be taken from them. And throw that worthless servant outside, into the darkness, where there will be weeping and gnashing of teeth" **(MATTHEW 25:14–30 NIV).**

The main focus of this parable that Jesus taught is on using the gifts God gives Christians to serve him while here on earth. But it also illustrates the need to invest money wisely for gain, rather than doing nothing with it.

Leaving an Inheritance

A good person leaves an inheritance for their children's children, but a sinner's wealth is stored up for the righteous. **(PROVERBS 13:22 NIV)**

An inheritance claimed too soon will not be blessed at the end. **(PROVERBS 20:21 NIV)**

Sometimes inherited money leads to laziness and a lack of appreciation for what a person has.

CHAPTER

5

LEARNING ABOUT LOANS

In Shakespeare's *Hamlet,* Polonius offered this sage advice to his son, who was going off to Paris: "Neither a borrower nor a lender be. For loan oft loses both itself and friend, And borrowing dulls the edge of husbandry [economy]." His advice is still good today. One almost sure way to wreck a relationship is to lend money to or borrow from a family member or friend.

Despite the high possibility of loans becoming messy, God doesn't ask you to avoid loans altogether. But he does give guidelines for borrowing and lending money.

Borrowing Money

The wicked borrow and do not repay, but the righteous give generously. (PSALM 37:21 NIV)

Although you shouldn't expect a loan to be repaid, if you borrow money, God expects you to repay it.

◆────────◆

The rich rule over the poor, and the borrower is slave to the lender. (PROVERBS 22:7 NIV)

As King Solomon wrote, borrowing money puts you into bondage to the lender.

◆────────◆

Give to everyone what you owe them: If you owe taxes, pay taxes; if revenue, then revenue; if respect, then respect; if honor, then honor. Let no debt remain outstanding, except the continuing debt to love one another, for whoever loves others has fulfilled the law. (ROMANS 13:7–8 NIV)

Paul, in writing to the Christians in Rome, told them to pay what they owe other people, including loans.

Lending Money

If you lend money to one of my people among you who is needy, do not treat it like a business deal; charge no interest. (EXODUS 22:25 NIV)

◆────────◆

If any of your fellow Israelites become poor and are unable to support themselves among you, help them as you would a foreigner and stranger, so they can continue to live among you. Do not take interest or any profit from them, but fear your God, so that they may continue to live among you. You must not lend them money at interest or sell them food at a profit. **(LEVITICUS 25:35–37** NIV**)**

If anyone is poor among your fellow Israelites in any of the towns of the land the LORD your God is giving you, do not be hardhearted or tightfisted toward them. Rather, be openhanded and freely lend them whatever they need. **(DEUTERONOMY 15:7–8** NIV**)**

Do not charge a fellow Israelite interest, whether on money or food or anything else that may earn interest. You may charge a foreigner interest, but not a fellow Israelite, so that the LORD your God may bless you in everything you put your hand to in the land you are entering to possess. **(DEUTERONOMY 23:19–20** NIV**)**

I pondered them in my mind and then accused the nobles and officials. I told them, "You are charging your own people interest!" So I called together a large meeting to deal with them and said: "As far as possible, we have bought back our fellow Jews who were sold to the Gentiles. Now you are selling your own people, only for them to be sold back to us!" They kept quiet, because they could find nothing to say. So I continued, "What you are doing is not right. Shouldn't you walk in the fear of our God to avoid the reproach of our Gentile enemies? I and my brothers and my men are also lending the people money and grain. But let us stop charging interest!" **(NEHEMIAH 5:7–10** NIV**)**.

When a later generation of Israelites broke God's command, Nehemiah reprimanded his fellow countrymen for charging interest on loans.

LORD, who may dwell in your sacred tent? Who may live on your holy mountain? The one whose walk is blameless, who does what is righteous, who speaks the truth from their heart . . . who lends money to the poor without interest; who does not accept a bribe against the innocent. Whoever does these things will never be shaken. **(PSALM 15:1–2, 5** NIV**)**

I was young and now I am old, yet I have never seen the righteous forsaken or their children begging bread. They are always generous and lend freely; their children will be a blessing. **(PSALM 37:25–26** NIV**)**

Good comes to those who lend money generously and conduct their business fairly. **(PSALM 112:5** NLT**)**

Lending money to people in need is a good deed that God will reward—although not necessarily financially.

Whoever is kind to the poor lends to the LORD, and he will reward them for what they have done. **(PROVERBS 19:17** NIV**)**

He who increases his wealth by interest and usury gathers it for him who is gracious to the poor. **(PROVERBS 28:8 NASB)**

If someone charges an excessive amount of interest on a loan, that person won't profit from it. God will make sure it ends up with the poor anyway.

Suppose there is a righteous man who does what is just and right. . . . He does not oppress anyone, but returns what he took in pledge for a loan. He does not commit robbery but gives his food to the hungry and provides clothing for the naked. He does not lend to them at interest or take a profit from them. He withholds his hand from doing wrong and judges fairly between two parties. He follows my decrees and faithfully keeps my laws. That man is righteous; he will surely live, declares the Sovereign LORD. . . . He lends at interest and takes a profit. Will such a man live? He will not! Because he has done all these detestable things, he is to be put to death; his blood will be on his own head. **(EZEKIEL 18:5, 7–9, 13 NIV)**

Give to the one who asks you, and do not turn away from the one who wants to borrow from you. **(MATTHEW 5:42 NIV)**

Was Jesus teaching that you should lend money for every request that comes your way, regardless of what it's for? Based on the rest of Scripture, most commentators would say no. He expects you to use discernment and give loans for genuine needs, not selfish or foolish requests.

When you make a loan to your neighbor, don't go into his house to take a security deposit. Wait outside, and the person to whom you're making the loan will bring the deposit out to you. If the person is poor, don't keep the coat you took as a deposit overnight. Make sure you bring it back to him at sunset. When he wears his coat to bed that night, he'll bless you. You will have done the right thing in the presence of the Lord your God. **(DEUTERONOMY 24:10–13 GOD'S WORD)**

And if you lend to those from whom you expect repayment, what credit is that to you? Even sinners lend to sinners, expecting to be repaid in full. But love your enemies, do good to them, and lend to them without expecting to get anything back. Then your reward will be great, and you will be children of the Most High, because he is kind to the ungrateful and wicked. **(LUKE 6:34–35 NIV)**

If you consider a loan to be a gift, you won't be disappointed when the borrower doesn't repay it. Plus you'll be following God's example of how he treats us generously.

Jubilee

The Lord spoke to Moses on Mount Sinai, "Tell the Israelites: When you come into the land I'm giving you, the land will celebrate a year to honor the Lord. Then, for six years you may plant crops in your fields, prune your vineyards, and gather what they produce. However, the seventh year will be a festival year for the land. It will be a year to honor the Lord. Don't plant crops in your fields or prune your vineyards. Don't harvest what grows by itself or harvest grapes from your vines. That year will be a festival for the land. Whatever the land produces during that year is for all of you to eat—for you, your male and female slaves, your hired workers, foreigners among you, your animals and the wild animals in your land. Everything the land produces will be yours to eat.

"Count seven of these years seven times for a total of 49 years. On the tenth day of the seventh month, the special day for the payment for sin, sound rams' horns throughout the country. Set apart the fiftieth year as holy, and proclaim liberty to everyone living in the land. This is your jubilee year. Every slave will be freed in order to return to his property and to his family. That fiftieth year will be your jubilee year. Don't plant or harvest what grows by itself or pick grapes from the vines in the land. The jubilee year will be holy to you. You will eat what the field itself produces.

"In this jubilee year every slave will be freed in order to return to his property. If you sell anything to your neighbor or buy anything from him, don't take advantage of him. When you buy property from your neighbor, take into account the number of years since the jubilee. Your neighbor must sell it to you taking into account the number of crops until the next jubilee. If there are still many years until the jubilee, you will pay more for it. If there are only a few years until the jubilee, you will pay less for it because he is selling you only the number of crops. Never take advantage of each other. Fear your God, because I am the Lord your God.

"Obey my laws, and carefully follow my rules. Then you will live securely in the land. The land will give you its products, and you will eat all you want and live there securely. You may ask, 'What will we eat in the seventh year if we do not plant or bring in our crops?' I will give you my blessing in the sixth year so that the land will produce enough for three years. You will plant again in the eighth year but live on what the land already produced. You will eat it, even in the ninth year, until the land produces more.

"Land must never be sold permanently, because the land is mine. To me you are strangers without permanent homes. People must always have the right to buy their property back. If your brother becomes poor and sells some of his property, then the one who can assume responsibility, his nearest relative, must buy back what he sold. If a man doesn't have anyone to buy it back for him, but if he prospers and earns enough to buy it back himself, he must count the years from its sale. Then he will pay what is left to the man to whom he sold it, and it will be his property again. However, if he cannot earn enough to buy it back, what he sold stays in the hands of the buyer until the year of jubilee. In the jubilee it will be released, and he will own it again.

"If anyone sells a home in a walled city, for one year after selling it he has the right to buy it back. He may buy it back only within that time. If he does not buy it back during that year, the house in the city belongs to the buyer for generations to come. It will not be released in the jubilee. However, houses in villages without walls are regarded as belonging to the fields of the land. They can be bought back. They will be released in the jubilee.

"The Levites always have the right to buy back their property in the cities they own. If any Levite buys back a house, in the jubilee the purchased house in the city will be released, because the houses in the Levite cities are their property among the Israelites. But a field that belongs to their cities must not be sold, because it is their permanent property.

"If an Israelite becomes poor and cannot support himself, help him. He must live with you as a stranger without a permanent home. Don't collect interest or make any profit from him. Fear your God by respecting other Israelites' lives. Never collect any kind of interest on your money or on the food you give them. I am the Lord your God, who brought you out of Egypt to give you Canaan and to be your God.

"If an Israelite becomes poor and sells himself to you, don't work him like a slave. He will be like a hired worker or a visitor to you. He may work with you until the year of jubilee. Then you will release him and his children to go back to their family and the property of their ancestors. They are my servants. I brought them out of Egypt. They must never be sold as slaves. Do not treat them harshly. Fear your God.

"You may have male and female slaves, but buy them from the nations around you. You may also buy them from the foreigners living among you and from their families born in your country. They will be your property. You may acquire them for yourselves and for your descendants as permanent property. You may work them as slaves. However, do not treat the Israelites harshly. They are your relatives.

"Someone who is a foreigner without a permanent home among you may become rich, and your relative living with him may be poor. The poor Israelite may sell himself to that foreigner or a member of his family. After he has sold himself, he has the right to be bought back. One of his brothers may buy him back. His uncle, his cousin, or some other relative could also buy him back. If he becomes rich, he could buy his own freedom. Then he and his buyer must take into account the number of years from the year he was bought until the year of jubilee. His sale price will be adjusted based on the number of years he was with his buyer, like the wages of a hired worker. If there are many years left, he must refund from his purchase price an amount equal to those years. If there are only a few years left until the year of jubilee, he must take them into account.

He must refund from his purchase price an amount equal to those years. During those years he should serve his buyer as a hired worker. His buyer should not treat him harshly. If he cannot buy his freedom in these ways, he and his children will be released in the year of jubilee.

"The Israelites belong to me as servants. They are my servants. I brought them out of Egypt. I am the Lord your God" (LEVITICUS 25 GOD'S WORD).

God cares very much for his people and his land, so he set up a special system in Israel so that these would not be exploited or ruined by unwise living. The year of jubilee allowed a portion of the Promised Land to return to the original owner God had given it to.

At the end of every seven years, you must cancel debts. This is what you will do: If you've made a loan, don't collect payment on the debt your neighbor still owes you. Don't demand that your neighbor or relative pay you, because the time for suspending payments on debts has been proclaimed in the Lord's honor. You may demand that a foreigner pay, but don't collect payment on the debt another Israelite still owes you. In any case, there shouldn't be any poor people among you, because the Lord your God will certainly bless you in the land he is giving you as your own possession. He will bless you only if you listen carefully to the Lord your God and faithfully obey all these commands I'm giving you today. The Lord your God will bless you, as he promised. You will make loans to many nations, but you will not have to borrow from any of them. You will rule many nations, but no nation will ever rule you.

This is what you must do whenever there are poor Israelites in one of your cities in the land that the Lord your God is giving you. Be generous to these poor people, and freely lend them as much as they need. Never be hard-hearted and tight-fisted with them.

When the seventh year—the year when payments on debts are canceled—is near, you might be stingy toward poor Israelites and give them nothing. Be careful not to think these worthless thoughts. The poor will complain to the Lord about you, and you will be condemned for your sin. Be sure to give to them without any hesitation. When you do this, the Lord your God will bless you in everything you work for and set out to do. There will always be poor people in the land. That's why I command you to be generous to other Israelites who are poor and needy.

Whenever Hebrew men or women are sold to you as slaves, they will be your slaves for six years. In the seventh year you must let them go free. But when you let them go, don't send them away empty-handed. Generously give them provisions— sheep from your flocks, grain from your threshing floor, and wine from your winepress. Be as generous to them as the Lord your God has been to you. Remember that you were slaves in Egypt and the Lord your God freed you. That's why I'm giving you this command today.

But suppose a male slave says to you, "I don't want to leave you," because he loves you and your family and is happy with you. Then take an awl and pierce it through his ear lobe into a door, and he will be your slave for life. Do the same to a female slave if she doesn't want to leave.

If you have to let your slave go free, it won't be a hardship for you. It would have cost you twice as much to hire someone to do the same work for those six years. Besides, the Lord your God will bless you in everything you do. **(DEUTERONOMY 15:1–18 GOD'S WORD)**

Cosigning Loans

My child, if you have put up security for a friend's debt or agreed to guarantee the debt of a stranger—if you have trapped yourself by your agreement and are caught by what you said—follow my advice and save yourself, for you have placed yourself at your friend's mercy. Now swallow your pride; go and beg to have your name erased. Don't put it off; do it now! Don't rest until you do. Save yourself like a gazelle escaping from a hunter, like a bird fleeing from a net. **(PROVERBS 6:1–5 NLT)**

There's danger in putting up security for a stranger's debt; it's safer not to guarantee another person's debt. **(PROVERBS 11:15 NLT)**

It's poor judgment to guarantee another person's debt or put up security for a friend. **(PROVERBS 17:18 NLT)**

Don't agree to guarantee another person's debt or put up security for someone else. **(PROVERBS 22:26 NLT)**

CHAPTER

6

DON'T BE GREEDY

You don't have to hunt for examples of greed. This strong desire to gain more and more money and things, and then do anything—including immoral and illegal actions—to get it, is everywhere.

For example, a company president gives himself a $500,000 raise while laying off a couple of dozen employees. Executives at an insurance company give themselves millions of dollars in bonuses while taking a government bailout to keep the company from declaring bankruptcy. An investment manager creates a giant Ponzi scheme to swindle people, and even charities, out of their savings with the lure of large returns (but of course the people who invested with him are also greedy for that gain).

Movie stars and sports figures make millions a year and fight for even more, when they're already making far more money than most of us.

Greed is one of the seven deadly sins, and the Bible has much to say about it.

If I have put my trust in gold or said to pure gold, "You are my security," if I have rejoiced over my great wealth, the fortune my hands had gained . . . then these also would be sins to be judged, for I would have been unfaithful to God on high. **(JOB 31:24–25, 28 NIV)**

In his arrogance the wicked man hunts down the weak, who are caught in the schemes he devises. He boasts about the cravings of his heart; he blesses the greedy and reviles the Lord. **(PSALM 10:2–3 NIV)**

Wicked people are full of themselves and scheme to get everything they want. They praise greed instead of God.

Incline my heart to your testimonies, and not to selfish gain! **(PSALM 119:36 ESV)**

If they say, "Come with us, let us lie in wait for blood; let us ambush the innocent without reason; like Sheol let us swallow them alive, and whole, like those who go down to the pit; we shall find all precious goods, we shall fill our houses with plunder; throw in your lot among us; we will all have one purse" my son, do not walk in the way with them; hold back your foot from their paths, for their feet run to evil, and they make haste to shed blood. For in vain is a net spread in the sight of any bird, but these men lie in wait for their own blood; they set an ambush for their own lives. Such are the ways of everyone who is greedy for unjust gain; it takes away the life of its possessors. **(PROVERBS 1:11–19 ESV)**

Solomon warned that people who do evil to satisfy their greed will reap what they sow and die as a result.

The greedy bring ruin to their households, but the one who hates bribes will live. **(PROVERBS 15:27 NIV)**

Some people are always greedy for more, but the godly love to give! **(PROVERBS 21:26 NLT)**

The greedy stir up conflict, but those who trust in the LORD will prosper. **(PROVERBS 28:25 NIV)**

A leech has twin daughters named "Gimme" and "Gimme more" **(PROVERBS 30:15 THE MESSAGE)**.

Greedy people, who are like bloodsucking insects, produce greedy children.

I turned my head and saw yet another wisp of smoke on its way to nothingness: a solitary person, completely alone—no children, no family, no friends—yet working obsessively late into the night, compulsively greedy for more and more, never bothering to ask, "Why am I working like a dog, never having any fun? And who cares?" More smoke. A bad business. **(ECCLESIASTES 4:7–8 THE MESSAGE)**

As goods increase, so do those who consume them. And what benefit are they to the owners except to feast their eyes on them? **(ECCLESIASTES 5:11 NIV)**

What sorrow for you who buy up house after house and field after field, until everyone is evicted and you live alone in the land. **(ISAIAH 5:8 NLT)**

Greed doesn't bring happiness. Instead, it results in loneliness.

Yes, they are greedy dogs which never have enough. And they are shepherds who cannot understand; they all look to their own way, every one for his own gain, from his own territory. **(ISAIAH 56:11 NKJV)**

Here Isaiah condemned leaders who satisfied their greed instead of watching out for the people entrusted to them.

I was enraged by their sinful greed; I punished them, and hid my face in anger, yet they kept on in their willful ways. **(ISAIAH 57:17 NIV)**

God calls greed a sin, which deserves punishment.

My people come to you, as they usually do, and sit before you to hear your words, but they do not put them into practice. Their mouths speak of love, but their hearts are greedy for unjust gain. **(EZEKIEL 33:31 NIV)**

God spoke these words to the prophet Ezekiel, warning him that some of his people would not obey Ezekiel's teaching because they were more concerned about satisfying their greedy desires.

For what is a man profited, if he shall gain the whole world, and lose his own soul? Or what shall a man give in exchange for his soul? **(MATTHEW 16:26 KJV)**

Your soul and its eternal destiny is worth far more than getting everything you want.

Jesus went into the temple courtyard and threw out everyone who was buying and selling there. He overturned the moneychangers' tables and the chairs of those who sold pigeons. He told them, "Scripture says, 'My house will be called a house of prayer,' but you're turning it into a gathering place for thieves!" **(MATTHEW 21:12–13 GOD'S WORD)**.

The temple should be a place of worship, not a place of greed. This event is also recorded in Mark and Luke (below).

When they came to Jerusalem, Jesus went into the temple courtyard and began to throw out those who were buying and selling there. He overturned the moneychangers' tables and the chairs of those who sold pigeons. He would not let anyone carry anything across the temple courtyard.

Then he taught them by saying, "Scripture says, 'My house will be called a house of prayer for all nations,' but you have turned it into a gathering place for thieves."

When the chief priests and scribes heard him, they looked for a way to kill him. They were afraid of him because he amazed all the crowds with his teaching. (Every evening Jesus and his disciples would leave the city.) (MARK 11:15–19 GOD'S WORD)

Jesus went into the temple courtyard and began to throw out those who were selling things there. He said to them, "Scripture says, 'My house will be a house of prayer,' but you have turned it into a gathering place for thieves."

Jesus taught in the temple courtyard every day. The chief priests, the scribes, and the leaders of the people looked for a way to kill him. But they could not find a way to do it, because all the people were eager to hear him. (LUKE 19:45–48 GOD'S WORD)

And the Lord said to him, "Now you Pharisees cleanse the outside of the cup and of the dish, but inside you are full of greed and wickedness" (LUKE 11:39 ESV).

Jesus condemned the religious leaders for their greed, which comes from the heart.

64

Then [Jesus] said to them, "Beware, and be on your guard against every form of greed; for not even when one has an abundance does his life consist of his possessions."

And He told them a parable, saying, "The land of a rich man was very productive. And he began reasoning to himself, saying, 'What shall I do, since I have no place to store my crops?'

"Then he said, 'This is what I will do: I will tear down my barns and build larger ones, and there I will store all my grain and my goods.

"'And I will say to my soul, "Soul, you have many goods laid up for many years to come; take your ease, eat, drink and be merry."'

"But God said to him, 'You fool! This very night your soul is required of you; and now who will own what you have prepared?'

"So is the man who stores up treasure for himself, and is not rich toward God" **(LUKE 12:15–21 NASB).**

———⋆⋆———

Then Jesus said, "A man had two sons. The younger son said to his father, 'Father, give me my share of the property.' So the father divided his property between his two sons.

"After a few days, the younger son gathered his possessions and left for a country far away from home. There he wasted everything he had on a wild lifestyle. He had nothing left when a severe famine spread throughout that country. He had nothing to live on. So he got a job from someone in that country and was sent to feed pigs in the fields. No one in the country would give him any food, and he was so hungry that he would have eaten what the pigs were eating.

"Finally, he came to his senses. He said, 'How many of my father's hired men have more food than they can eat, while I'm starving to death here? I'll go at once to my father, and I'll say to him, "Father, I've sinned against heaven and you. I don't deserve to be called your son anymore. Make me one of your hired men."'

"So he went at once to his father. While he was still at a distance, his father saw him and felt sorry for him. He ran to his son, put his arms around him, and kissed him. Then his son said to him, 'Father, I've sinned against heaven and you. I don't deserve to be called your son anymore.'

"The father said to his servants, 'Hurry! Bring out the best robe, and put it on him. Put a ring on his finger and sandals on his feet. Bring the fattened calf, kill it, and let's celebrate with a feast. My son was dead and has come back to life. He was lost but has been found.' Then they began to celebrate.

"His older son was in the field. As he was coming back to the house, he heard music and dancing. He called to one of the servants and asked what was happening.

"The servant told him, 'Your brother has come home. So your father has killed the fattened calf to celebrate your brother's safe return.'

"Then the older son became angry and wouldn't go into the house. His father came out and begged him to come in. But he answered his father, 'All these years I've worked like a slave for you. I've never disobeyed one of your commands. Yet, you've never given me so much as a little goat for a celebration with my friends. But this son of yours spent your money on prostitutes, and when he came home, you killed the fattened calf for him.'

"His father said to him, 'My child, you're always with me. Everything I have is yours. But we have something to celebrate, something to be happy about. This brother of yours was dead but has come back to life. He was lost but has been found' " (LUKE 15:11–32 GOD'S WORD).

In the well-known parable of the prodigal son, both the younger and the older son struggle with greed. The good news is that God will forgive us if we repent.

And just as they did not see fit to acknowledge God any longer, God gave them over to a depraved mind, to do those things which are not proper, being filled with all unrighteousness, wickedness, greed, evil; full of envy, murder, strife, deceit, malice; they are gossips. (ROMANS 1:28–29 NASB)

Greed is one of many sins that results from rejecting God.

So this I say, and affirm together with the Lord, that you walk no longer just as the Gentiles also walk, in the futility of their mind, being darkened in their understanding, excluded from the life of God because of the ignorance that is in them, because of the hardness of their heart; and they, having become callous, have given themselves over to sensuality for the practice of every kind of impurity with greediness. (EPHESIANS 4:17–19 NASB)

Put to death, therefore, whatever belongs to your earthly nature: sexual immorality, impurity, lust, evil desires and greed, which is idolatry. (COLOSSIANS 3:5 NIV)

Paul equated greed with idolatry, worshiping something other than God.

A bishop then must be blameless, the husband of one wife, temperate, sober-minded, of good behavior, hospitable, able to teach; not given to wine, not violent, not greedy for money, but gentle, not quarrelsome, not covetous. **(1 TIMOTHY 3:2–3 NKJV)**

For there are many rebellious people who engage in useless talk and deceive others. This is especially true of those who insist on circumcision for salvation. They must be silenced, because they are turning whole families away from the truth by their false teaching. And they do it only for money. **(TITUS 1:10–11 NLT)**

Paul warned Titus about religious people who teach false doctrine because they are greedy and hope to gain financially from such teaching.

But false prophets also arose among the people, just as there will also be false teachers among you, who will secretly introduce destructive heresies, even denying the Master who bought them, bringing swift destruction upon themselves. Many will follow their sensuality, and because of them the way of the truth will be maligned; and in their greed they will exploit you with false words; their judgment from long ago is not idle, and their destruction is not asleep. **(2 PETER 2:1–3 NASB)**

Shepherd the flock of God among you, exercising oversight not under compulsion, but voluntarily, according to the

will of God; and not for sordid gain, but with eagerness.
(1 PETER 5:2 NASB)

Paul told pastors to take care of the people in their congregations to please God, not for greed.

CHAPTER

7

GIVING GENEROUSLY TO OTHERS

W hen you hear the name Oprah Winfrey, you probably think first of her Emmy Award-winning television talk show. *The Oprah Winfrey Show* was on the air for twenty-five years, exploring lifestyle and social issues, promoting a variety of religious beliefs, encouraging viewers to read more through her book club, and interviewing celebrities.

You might remember that she was nominated for an Academy Award for her role in *The Color Purple* and she publishes a magazine, *O, The Oprah Magazine*.

She is also one of the most influential and richest people in the world, as well as a top-ranking philanthropist.[1] Through Oprah's Angel Network, she funds scholarships and women's and youth shelters. According to BusinessPundit.com, she gives away around $50 million a year for children's, women's, and families' education.

Sure, it's easy to give away that much money when your net worth is $2.7 billion.[2] But the Bible teaches that everyone can—and should—give generously to others, no matter what their net worth is.

If anyone is poor among your fellow Israelites in any of the towns of the land the LORD your God is giving you, do not be hardhearted or tightfisted toward them. Rather, be openhanded and freely lend them whatever they need. . . . Give generously to them and do so without a grudging heart; then because of this the LORD your God will bless you in all your work and in everything you put your hand to. **(DEUTERONOMY 15:7–8, 10 NIV)**

Do not withhold good from those to whom it is due, when it is in your power to do it. Do not say to your neighbor, "Go, and come again, tomorrow I will give it"—when you have it with you. **(PROVERBS 3:27–28 ESV)**

One person gives freely, yet gains even more; another withholds unduly, but comes to poverty. A generous person will prosper; whoever refreshes others will be refreshed. **(PROVERBS 11:24–25 NIV)**

Beware of practicing your righteousness before men to be noticed by them; otherwise you have no reward with your Father who is in heaven.

So when you give to the poor, do not sound a trumpet before you, as the hypocrites do in the synagogues and in the streets, so that they may be honored by men. Truly I say to you, they have their reward in full.

But when you give to the poor, do not let your left hand know what your right hand is doing, so that your giving will be in secret; and your Father who sees what is done in secret will reward you. **(MATTHEW 6:1–4 NASB)**

Jesus taught that you shouldn't make a show of your giving, drawing attention to what you are doing.

Soon afterward [Jesus] went on through cities and villages, proclaiming and bringing the good news of the kingdom of God. And the twelve were with him, and also some women who had been healed of evil spirits and infirmities: Mary, called Magdalene, from whom seven demons had gone out, and Joanna, the wife of Chuza, Herod's household manager, and Susanna, and many others, who provided for them out of their means. **(LUKE 8:1–3 ESV)**

Jesus and his twelve disciples did not have to find work while they were teaching and helping people because women who had money generously supported them.

Jesus replied, "A man was going down from Jerusalem to Jericho, and he fell among robbers, who stripped him and beat him and departed, leaving him half dead. Now by chance a priest was going down that road, and when he saw him he passed by on the other side. So likewise a Levite, when he came to the place and saw him, passed by on the other side. But a Samaritan, as he journeyed, came to where he was, and when he saw him, he had compassion. He went to him and bound up his wounds, pouring on oil and wine. Then he set him on his own animal and brought him to an inn and took care of him. And the next day he took out two denarii and gave them to the innkeeper, saying, 'Take care of him, and whatever more you spend, I will repay you when I come back'" **(LUKE 10:30–35 ESV).**

Samaritans and Jewish people hated each other. But the Samaritan was the one who gave money and time to help a Jewish man beaten by robbers.

And all the believers met together in one place and shared everything they had. They sold their property and possessions and shared the money with those in need. **(ACTS 2:44–45 NLT)**

The first Christians were very generous with one another, meeting the needs of their brothers and sisters in Christ.

All the believers were united in heart and mind. And they felt that what they owned was not their own, so they shared everything they had. . . . There were no needy people among them, because those who owned land or houses would sell them and bring the money to the apostles to give to those in need. **(ACTS 4:32, 34–35 NLT)**

So the believers in Antioch decided to send relief to the brothers and sisters in Judea, everyone giving as much as they could. (ACTS 11:29 NLT)

And I have been a constant example of how you can help those in need by working hard. You should remember the words of the Lord Jesus: "It is more blessed to give than to receive" (ACTS 20:35 NLT).

Having then gifts differing according to the grace that is given to us, let us use them: . . . he who gives, with liberality. (ROMANS 12:6, 8 NKJV)

When God's people are in need, be ready to help them. Always be ready to practice hospitality. (ROMANS 12:13 NLT)

Now regarding your question about the money being collected for God's people in Jerusalem. You should follow the same procedure I gave to the churches in Galatia. On the first day of each week, you should each put aside a portion of the money you have earned. Don't wait until I get there and then try to collect it all at once. (1 CORINTHIANS 16:1–2 NLT)

And now, brothers and sisters, we want you to know about the grace that God has given the Macedonian churches. In the midst of a very severe trial, their overflowing joy and their extreme poverty welled up in rich generosity. For I testify that they gave as much as they were able, and even beyond their ability. Entirely on their own, they urgently pleaded with us for the privilege of sharing in this service to the Lord's people. And they exceeded our expectations: They gave themselves first of all to the Lord, and then by the will of God also to us. . . .

Our desire is not that others might be relieved while you are hard pressed, but that there might be equality. At the present time your plenty will supply what they need, so that in turn their plenty will supply what you need. The goal is equality, as it is written: "The one who gathered much did not have too much, and the one who gathered little did not have too little" (2 CORINTHIANS 8:1–5, 13–15 NIV).

Remember this: Whoever sows sparingly will also reap sparingly, and whoever sows generously will also reap generously. Each of you should give what you have decided in your heart to give, not reluctantly or under compulsion, for God loves a cheerful giver. And God is able to bless you abundantly, so that in all things at all times, having all that you need, you will abound in every good work. As it is written: "They have freely scattered their gifts to the poor; their righteousness endures forever."

Now he who supplies seed to the sower and bread for food will also supply and increase your store of seed and will enlarge the harvest of your righteousness. You will be enriched in every way so that you can be generous on every occasion, and through us your generosity will result in thanksgiving to God.

This service that you perform is not only supplying the needs of the Lord's people but is also overflowing in many expressions of thanks to God. Because of the service by which you have proved yourselves, others will praise God for the obedience that accompanies your confession of the gospel of Christ, and for your generosity in sharing with them and with everyone else. And in their prayers for you their hearts will go out to you, because of the surpassing grace God has given you. Thanks be to God for his indescribable gift! **(2 CORINTHIANS 9:6–15 NIV)**

If you are a thief, quit stealing. Instead, use your hands for good hard work, and then give generously to others in need. **(EPHESIANS 4:28 NLT)**

But do not forget to do good and to share, for with such sacrifices God is well pleased. **(HEBREWS 13:16 NKJV)**

Suppose you see a brother or sister who has no food or clothing, and you say, "Good-bye and have a good day; stay warm and eat well"—but then you don't give that person any food or clothing. What good does that do? **(JAMES 2:15–16 NLT)**

But whoever has this world's goods, and sees his brother in need, and shuts up his heart from him, how does the love of God abide in him? **(1 JOHN 3:17 NKJV)**

TITHING AND GIVING TO GOD'S WORK

I f every church member and regular attendee gave at least ten percent of his or her income, the church would never lack money for its ministries and the missionaries it supports. Unfortunately, too many people give too little back to God without knowing that it's to their spiritual detriment.

God doesn't need our money. After all, he owns everything, as pointed out in chapter 1. But he asks believers to give a portion of their money back to him as an act of worship and obedience. The Bible elaborates on this truth.

Then the LORD spoke to Moses, saying: "Speak to the children of Israel, that they bring Me an offering. From everyone who gives it willingly with his heart you shall take My offering" (EXODUS 25:1–2 NKJV).

Then Moses said to the whole Israelite community, "This is what the LORD has commanded: Choose something of your own to give as a special contribution to the LORD. Let everyone who is willing bring this kind of contribution to the LORD: gold, silver, and bronze, violet, purple, and bright red yarn, fine linen, goats' hair, rams' skins dyed red, fine leather, acacia wood, olive oil for the lamps, spices for the anointing oil and for the sweet-smelling incense, onyx stones, and other precious stones to be set in the chief priest's ephod and breastplate. (EXODUS 35:4–9 GOD'S WORD)

In addition to specific tithes, there were also times in which God asked the Israelites to give extra out of their abundance.

Moses turned over to them all the contributions the Israelites had brought for the work of constructing the holy place. But the people still kept bringing him freewill offerings every morning. Finally, all the skilled craftsmen who were working on the holy place stopped what they were doing. They all came to Moses. They said, "The people are bringing much more than we need for doing the work the LORD commanded us to do."

So Moses gave instructions to have the following message announced all over camp: "No man or woman needs to make anything more to give as their special contribution to the holy place." Then the people stopped bringing gifts.

The material they had was more than enough to do the job.
(EXODUS 36:3–7 GOD'S WORD)

At this point in Israel's history, the people gave generously.

Every tenth of the land's produce, grain from the soil or fruit from the trees, belongs to the LORD; it is holy to the LORD. If a man decides to redeem any part of this tenth, he must add one-fifth to its value. Every tenth animal from the herd or flock, which passes under the [shepherd's] rod, will be holy to the LORD. (LEVITICUS 27:30–32 HCSB)

As Moses taught, a tenth (tithe) of everything earned, including money, crops, and animals, belongs to the Lord.

Every year be sure to save a tenth of the crops harvested from whatever you plant in your fields. Eat the tenth of your grain, new wine, and olive oil, and eat the firstborn of your cattle, sheep, and goats in the presence of the LORD your God in the place he will choose to put his name. Then you will learn to fear the LORD your God as long as you live.

But the place the LORD your God will choose to put his name may be too far away. He may bless you with so much that you can't carry a tenth of your income that far. If so, exchange the tenth part of your income for silver. Take the silver with you, and go to the place the LORD your God will choose. Use the silver to buy whatever you want: cattle, sheep, goats, wine, liquor—whatever you choose. Then you and your family will eat and enjoy yourselves there in the presence of the LORD your God. Never forget to take care of the Levites who live in your cities. They have no land of their own as you have.

At the end of every third year bring a tenth of that year's crop, and store it in your cities. Foreigners, orphans, and widows who live in your cities may come to eat all they want. The Levites may also come because they have no land of their own as you have. Then the LORD your God will bless you in whatever work you do. **(DEUTERONOMY 14:22–29 GOD'S WORD)**

Honor the LORD from your wealth and from the first of all your produce; So your barns will be filled with plenty and your vats will overflow with new wine. **(PROVERBS 3:9–10 NASB)**

Giving an offering to God should be the first expenditure from your money, rather than giving out of what is left over after paying the bills.

"Is it a time for you yourselves to be living in your paneled houses, while this house remains a ruin?"

Now this is what the LORD Almighty says: "Give careful thought to your ways. You have planted much, but harvested little. You eat, but never have enough. You drink, but never have your fill. You put on clothes, but are not warm. You earn wages, only to put them in a purse with holes in it" **(HAGGAI 1:4–6 NIV)**.

Through the prophet Haggai, God told his people not to be focused on their own interests instead of on the Lord.

"Will a man rob God? Yet you have robbed Me! But you say, 'In what way have we robbed You?' In tithes and offerings. You are cursed with a curse, for you have robbed Me, even this whole nation. Bring all the tithes into the storehouse, that there may be food in My house, and try Me now in this," says the LORD of hosts, "If I will not open for you the windows of heaven and pour out for you such blessing that there will not be room enough to receive it.

"And I will rebuke the devourer for your sakes, so that he will not destroy the fruit of your ground, nor shall the vine fail to bear fruit for you in the field," says the LORD of hosts. **(MALACHI 3:8–11 NKJV)**

The Old Testament tithe was more than ten percent of what the land and livestock produced. A system of tithes, averaging more than 23 percent, was part of God's law given to Moses (Leviticus 27:30–33; Numbers 18:21–32; Deuteronomy 12:6; 14:22–29; 26:12). The equivalent of the storehouse in Malachi's day is the church where you worship.

What sorrow awaits you teachers of religious law and you Pharisees. Hypocrites! For you are careful to tithe even the tiniest income from your herb gardens, but you ignore the more important aspects of the law—justice, mercy, and faith. You should tithe, yes, but do not neglect the more important things. **(MATTHEW 23:23 NLT)**

Jesus sat down near the collection box in the Temple and watched as the crowds dropped in their money. Many rich people put in large amounts. Then a poor widow came and dropped in two small coins.

Jesus called his disciples to him and said, "I tell you the truth, this poor widow has given more than all the others who are making contributions. For they gave a tiny part of their surplus, but she, poor as she is, has given everything she had to live on" (MARK 12:41–44 NLT).

Jesus was in Bethany in the home of Simon, a man who had suffered from a skin disease. While Jesus was sitting there, a woman went to him with a bottle of very expensive perfume and poured it on his head.

The disciples were irritated when they saw this. They asked, "Why did she waste it like this? It could have been sold for a high price, and the money could have been given to the poor."

Since Jesus knew what was going on, he said to them, "Why are you bothering this woman? She has done a beautiful thing for me. You will always have the poor with you, but you will not always have me with you. She poured this perfume on my body before it is placed in a tomb. I can guarantee this truth: Wherever this Good News is spoken in the world, what she has done will also be told in memory of her" (MATTHEW 26:6–13 GOD'S WORD).

We should use our money to glorify God. There will always be other needs, but we must not neglect giving to the Lord.

Give, and you will receive. Your gift will return to you in full—pressed down, shaken together to make room for more, running over, and poured into your lap. The amount you give will determine the amount you get back. (LUKE 6:38 NLT)

On the first day of the week, each of you is to set something aside and save to the extent that he prospers, so that no collections will need to be made when I come. (1 CORINTHIANS 16:2 HCSB)

Every Christian is responsible for giving proportional to his or her income, as well as giving systematically and regularly.

Remember this—a farmer who plants only a few seeds will get a small crop. But the one who plants generously will get a generous crop. You must each decide in your heart how much to give. And don't give reluctantly or in response to pressure. "For God loves a person who gives cheerfully." And God will generously provide all you need. Then you will always have everything you need and plenty left over to share with others. (2 CORINTHIANS 9:6–8 NLT)

THERE'S NO SHAME IN BEING POOR

Have you ever visited a developing country? If so, you may have been tempted to turn your eyes from the overwhelming poverty. But we need to be aware of how the poor live. It's sometimes hard to imagine how people, including little children, can survive with no bathrooms, no running water, no comfortable furniture, no electricity, no computers, no microwaves, no refrigerators, no heat when the sun goes down and the temperature drops.

About half of the world's population live on less than $2.50 a day, the definition of poverty.[3] Even in the United States, the richest country in the world, almost fifteen percent of residents live in poverty.[4]

Does God care for the poor? What is our responsibility toward the poor? What does the Bible have to say on this subject?

God's Concern for the Poor

The LORD sends poverty and wealth; he humbles and he exalts. **(1 SAMUEL 2:7** NIV**)**

Is he not the One who says to kings, "You are worthless," and to nobles, "You are wicked," who shows no partiality to princes and does not favor the rich over the poor, for they are all the work of his hands? **(JOB 34:18–19** NIV**)**

They caused the cry of the poor to come before him, so that he heard the cry of the needy. **(JOB 34:28** NIV**)**

"Because the poor are plundered and the needy groan, I will now arise," says the LORD. "I will protect them from those who malign them" **(PSALM 12:5** NIV**)**.

You evildoers frustrate the plans of the poor, but the LORD is their refuge. **(PSALM 14:6** NIV**)**

My whole being will exclaim, "Who is like you, LORD? You rescue the poor from those too strong for them, the poor and needy from those who rob them" **(PSALM 35:10** NIV**)**.

Your people settled in it, and from your bounty, God, you provided for the poor. **(PSALM 68:10** NIV**)**

He raises the poor from the dust and lifts the needy from the ash heap. **(PSALM 113:7 NIV)**

I know that the LORD secures justice for the poor and upholds the cause of the needy. **(PSALM 140:12 NIV)**

Rich and poor have this in common: The LORD is the Maker of them all. **(PROVERBS 22:2 NIV)**

The poor and the oppressor have this in common: The LORD gives sight to the eyes of both. **(PROVERBS 29:13 NIV)**

You have been a refuge for the poor, a refuge for the needy in their distress, a shelter from the storm and a shade from the heat. **(ISAIAH 25:4 NIV)**

Right Actions Toward the Poor

Do not pervert justice; do not show partiality to the poor or favoritism to the great, but judge your neighbor fairly. **(LEVITICUS 19:15 NIV)**

If any of your fellow Israelites become poor and are unable to support themselves among you, help them as you would a foreigner and stranger, so they can continue to live among you. **(LEVITICUS 25:35 NIV)**

If anyone is poor among your fellow Israelites in any of the towns of the land the LORD your God is giving you, do not be hardhearted or tightfisted toward them. Rather, be open-handed and freely lend them whatever they need. Be careful not to harbor this wicked thought: "The seventh year, the year for canceling debts, is near," so that you do not show ill will toward the needy among your fellow Israelites and give them nothing. They may then appeal to the LORD against you, and you will be found guilty of sin. Give generously to them and do so without a grudging heart; then because of this the LORD your God will bless you in all your work and in everything you put your hand to.

There will always be poor people in the land. Therefore I command you to be openhanded toward your fellow Israelites who are poor and needy in your land. (DEUTERONOMY 15:7–11 NIV)

Whoever heard me spoke well of me, and those who saw me commended me, because I rescued the poor who cried for help, and the fatherless who had none to assist them. (JOB 29:11–12 NIV)

This is Job's testimony when he responded to his so-called friends' accusations.

Have I not wept for those in trouble? Has not my soul grieved for the poor? (JOB 30:25 NIV)

This verse is also part of Job's testimony.

This is what you must do when you're harvesting wheat in your field. If you forget to bring in one of the bundles of wheat, don't go back to get it. Leave it there for foreigners, orphans, and widows. Then the Lord your God will bless you in everything you do.

When you harvest olives from your trees, never knock down all of them. Leave some for foreigners, orphans, and widows.

When you pick the grapes in your vineyard, don't pick all of them. Leave some for foreigners, orphans, and widows. **(DEUTERONOMY 24:19–21 GOD'S WORD)**

Those who have plenty should be aware of the needs of the poor, giving them opportunities to earn a living.

Blessed is he who considers the poor; the LORD will deliver him in time of trouble. **(PSALM 41:1 NKJV)**

Defend the weak and the fatherless; uphold the cause of the poor and the oppressed. **(PSALM 82:3 NIV)**

They have freely scattered their gifts to the poor, their righteousness endures forever; their horn will be lifted high in honor. **(PSALM 112:9 NIV)**

Whoever despises his neighbor is a sinner, but blessed is he who is generous to the poor. . . . Whoever oppresses a poor man insults his Maker, but he who is generous to the needy honors him. **(PROVERBS 14:21, 31 ESV)**

91

Better the poor whose walk is blameless than a fool whose lips are perverse. **(PROVERBS 19:1** NIV**)**

Whoever is kind to the poor lends to the LORD, and he will reward them for what they have done. **(PROVERBS 19:17** NIV**)**

The generous will themselves be blessed, for they share their food with the poor. **(PROVERBS 22:9** NIV**)**

Better the poor whose walk is blameless than the rich whose ways are perverse. **(PROVERBS 28:6** NIV**)**

Those who give to the poor will lack nothing, but those who close their eyes to them receive many curses. **(PROVERBS 28:27** NIV**)**

The righteous care about justice for the poor, but the wicked have no such concern. **(PROVERBS 29:7** NIV**)**

If a king judges the poor with fairness, his throne will be established forever. **(PROVERBS 29:14** NIV**)**

She opens her arms to the poor and extends her hands to the needy. **(PROVERBS 31:20 NIV)**

This verse is part of the description of an excellent wife.

⁑

Is not this the kind of fasting I have chosen: to loose the chains of injustice and untie the cords of the yoke, to set the oppressed free and break every yoke? Is it not to share your food with the hungry and to provide the poor wanderer with shelter—when you see the naked, to clothe them, and not to turn away from your own flesh and blood? **(ISAIAH 58:6–7 NIV)**

These are God's words to Isaiah and his people.

⁑

He withholds his hand from mistreating the poor and takes no interest or profit from them. He keeps my laws and follows my decrees. He will not die for his father's sin; he will surely live. **(EZEKIEL 18:17 NIV)**

⁑

And the word of the LORD came again to Zechariah: "This is what the LORD Almighty said: 'Administer true justice; show mercy and compassion to one another. Do not oppress the widow or the fatherless, the foreigner or the poor. Do not plot evil against each other'" **(ZECHARIAH 7:8–10 NIV)**.

⁑

Jesus said, The poor you will always have with you, and you can help them any time you want. **(MARK 14:7 NIV)**

⁑

93

But now as for what is inside you—be generous to the poor, and everything will be clean for you. **(LUKE 11:41** NIV**)**

Jesus spoke these words to the religious leaders who were more concerned with their outward obedience to God's law than to the condition of their hearts.

But when you give a banquet, invite the poor, the crippled, the lame, the blind, and you will be blessed. Although they cannot repay you, you will be repaid at the resurrection of the righteous. **(LUKE 14:13–14** NIV**)**

For Macedonia and Achaia were pleased to make a contribution for the poor among the Lord's people in Jerusalem. **(ROMANS 15:26** NIV**)**

In Joppa there was a disciple named Tabitha (in Greek her name is Dorcas); she was always doing good and helping the poor. **(ACTS 9:36** NIV**)**

Tabitha provides an example to follow today.

Cornelius stared at the angel. He became afraid and said, "What do you want, Lord?"

The angel said, "God has heard your prayers. He has seen that you give to the poor, and he remembers you" **(ACTS 10:4** NCV**).**

God notices when you give to the poor.

Now, however, I am on my way to Jerusalem in the service of the Lord's people there. For Macedonia and Achaia were pleased to make a contribution for the poor among the Lord's people in Jerusalem. They were pleased to do it, and indeed they owe it to them. For if the Gentiles have shared in the Jews' spiritual blessings, they owe it to the Jews to share with them their material blessings. **(ROMANS 15:25–27 NIV)**

Paul wrote these words to the church in Rome.

It is written in the Scriptures: "He gives freely to the poor. The things he does are right and will continue forever" **(2 CORINTHIANS 9:9 NCV).**

All they asked was that we should continue to remember the poor, the very thing I had been eager to do all along. **(GALATIANS 2:10 NIV)**

Wrong Actions Toward the Poor

For [the godless person] has oppressed the poor and left them destitute; he has seized houses he did not build. **(JOB 20:19 NIV)**

The wealth of the rich is their fortress; the poverty of the poor is their destruction. **(PROVERBS 10:15 NLT)**

This proverb is a description of what the situation was in Solomon's time, not advice for what should happen.

A person's riches may ransom their life, but the poor cannot respond to threatening rebukes. **(PROVERBS 13:8 NIV)**

One advantage of not having anything is that people can't threaten to take away your possessions.

Whoever mistreats the poor insults their Maker; whoever enjoys someone's trouble will be punished. **(PROVERBS 17:5 NCV)**

The poor plead for mercy, but the rich answer harshly. **(PROVERBS 18:23 NIV)**

The relatives of the poor despise them; how much more will their friends avoid them! Though the poor plead with them, their friends are gone. **(PROVERBS 19:7 NLT)**

Whoever shuts their ears to the cry of the poor will also cry out and not be answered. **(PROVERBS 21:13 NIV)**

One who oppresses the poor to increase his wealth and one who gives gifts to the rich—both come to poverty. **(PROVERBS 22:16 NIV)**

Do not abuse poor people because they are poor, and do not take away the rights of the needy in court. The LORD will defend them in court and will take the life of those who take away their rights. **(PROVERBS 22:22–23 NCV)**

A ruler who oppresses the poor is like a driving rain that leaves no crops. **(PROVERBS 28:3 NIV)**

He oppresses the poor and needy. He commits robbery. He does not return what he took in pledge. He looks to the idols. He does detestable things. **(EZEKIEL 18:12 NIV)**

This is part of God's description of a violent son.

Even common people oppress the poor, rob the needy, and deprive foreigners of justice. "I looked for someone who might rebuild the wall of righteousness that guards the land. I searched for someone to stand in the gap in the wall so I wouldn't have to destroy the land, but I found no one. So now I will pour out my fury on them, consuming them with the fire of my anger. I will heap on their heads the full penalty for all their sins. I, the Sovereign Lord, have spoken!" **(EZEKIEL 22:29–31 NLT).**

Hear this, you who trample the needy and do away with the poor of the land, saying, "When will the New Moon be over that we may sell grain, and the Sabbath be ended that we may market wheat?"—skimping on the measure, boosting the price and cheating with dishonest scales, buying the poor with silver and the needy for a pair of sandals, selling even the sweepings with the wheat. **(AMOS 8:4–6 NIV)**

My dear brothers and sisters, as believers in our glorious Lord Jesus Christ, never think some people are more important than others. Suppose someone comes into your church meeting wearing nice clothes and a gold ring. At the same time a poor person comes in wearing old, dirty clothes. You show special attention to the one wearing nice clothes and say, "Please, sit here in this good seat." But you say to the poor person, "Stand over there," or, "Sit on the floor by my feet." What are you doing? You are making some people more important than others, and with evil thoughts you are deciding that one person is better.

Listen, my dear brothers and sisters! God chose the poor in the world to be rich with faith and to receive the kingdom God promised to those who love him. But you show no respect to the poor. The rich are always trying to control your lives. They are the ones who take you to court. And they are the ones who speak against Jesus, who owns you.

This royal law is found in the Scriptures: "Love your neighbor as you love yourself." If you obey this law, you are doing right. But if you treat one person as being more important than another, you are sinning. You are guilty of breaking God's law. (JAMES 2:1–9 NCV)

CHAPTER

10

YOU AND WEALTH

Given a choice, most people would choose to be rich. They dream about inheriting a million dollars, even if none of their relatives have that much. They spend money they often can't afford to lose on lottery tickets, hoping to win the big jackpot. They play slot machines and gamble at casino tables, sure they can double and triple their money. As Alexander Pope wrote, "Hope springs eternal."

Even when people win or inherit money, they want more. No matter how much money a person has, it's rarely enough. Millionaires confess they don't feel rich enough, although you'd probably change places with one any time.

Surprisingly, many lottery winners go bankrupt or encounter serious financial problems within five years of winning huge jackpots because they don't know how to handle wealth, and then they need more. It's a vicious cycle.

But what does the Bible say about wealth and how to deal with it?

Wealth Comes From God

God brings poverty and God brings wealth. (1 SAMUEL 2:7
THE MESSAGE)

[God] doesn't care how great a person may be, and he pays
no more attention to the rich than to the poor. He made them
all. (JOB 34:19 NLT)

Everyone also to whom God has given wealth and possessions
and power to enjoy them, and to accept his lot and rejoice in
his toil—this is the gift of God. (ECCLESIASTES 5:19 ESV)

Don't Trust in Wealth

If I have made gold my hope, or said to fine gold, "You are my
confidence"; if I have rejoiced because my wealth was great,
and because my hand had gained much. . . . This also would
be an iniquity deserving of judgment, for I would have denied
God who is above. (JOB 31:24–25, 28 NKJV)

Job avoided the temptation to trust in wealth instead of God.

If wealth increases, pay no attention to it. (PSALM 62:10 HCSB)

Whoever trusts in his riches will fall, but the righteous will
flourish like a green leaf. (PROVERBS 11:28 ESV)

Command those who are rich in this present age not to be haughty, nor to trust in uncertain riches but in the living God, who gives us richly all things to enjoy. **(1 TIMOTHY 6:17 NKJV)**

Wealth Doesn't Last

So don't be dismayed when the wicked grow rich and their homes become ever more splendid. For when they die, they take nothing with them. Their wealth will not follow them into the grave. In this life they consider themselves fortunate and are applauded for their success. But they will die like all before them and never again see the light of day. People who boast of their wealth don't understand; they will die, just like animals. **(PSALM 49:16–20 NLT)**

A thick bankroll is no help when life falls apart, but a principled life can stand up to the worst. **(PROVERBS 11:4 THE MESSAGE)**

In the blink of an eye wealth disappears, for it will sprout wings and fly away like an eagle. **(PROVERBS 23:5 NLT)**

And those who are rich should boast that God has humbled them. They will fade away like a little flower in the field. The hot sun rises and the grass withers; the little flower droops and falls, and its beauty fades away. In the same way, the rich will fade away with all of their achievements. **(JAMES 1:10–11 NLT)**

Look here, you rich people: Weep and groan with anguish because of all the terrible troubles ahead of you. Your wealth is rotting away, and your fine clothes are moth-eaten rags. Your gold and silver have become worthless. The very wealth you were counting on will eat away your flesh like fire. This treasure you have accumulated will stand as evidence against you on the day of judgment. For listen! Hear the cries of the field workers whom you have cheated of their pay. The wages you held back cry out against you. The cries of those who harvest your fields have reached the ears of the Lord of Heaven's Armies.

You have spent your years on earth in luxury, satisfying your every desire. You have fattened yourselves for the day of slaughter. You have condemned and killed innocent people who do not resist you. (JAMES 5:1–6 NLT)

Wealth Doesn't Count With God

They trust in their wealth and boast of their abundant riches. Yet these cannot redeem a person or pay his ransom to God. (PSALM 49:6–7 HCSB)

The righteous will see and fear; they will laugh at you, saying, "Here now is the man who did not make God his stronghold but trusted in his great wealth and grew strong by destroying others!" (PSALM 52:6–7 NIV).

Your silver and gold will not save you on that day of the Lord's anger. (ZEPHANIAH 1:18 NLT)

Wealth will not save anyone on judgment day.

What good will it be for someone to gain the whole world, yet forfeit their soul? Or what can anyone give in exchange for their soul? **(MATTHEW 16:26** NIV**)**

Then Jesus looked around and said to His disciples, "How hard it is for those who have riches to enter the kingdom of God!" And the disciples were astonished at His words. But Jesus answered again and said to them, "Children, how hard it is for those who trust in riches to enter the kingdom of God! It is easier for a camel to go through the eye of a needle than for a rich man to enter the kingdom of God."

And they were greatly astonished, saying among themselves, "Who then can be saved?"

But Jesus looked at them and said, "With men it is impossible, but not with God; for with God all things are possible" **(MARK 10:23–27** NKJV**)**.

Then [Jesus] spoke a parable to them, saying: "The ground of a certain rich man yielded plentifully. And he thought within himself, saying, 'What shall I do, since I have no room to store my crops?' So he said, 'I will do this: I will pull down my barns and build greater, and there I will store all my crops and my goods. And I will say to my soul, "Soul, you have many goods laid up for many years; take your ease; eat, drink, and be merry." ' But God said to him, 'Fool! This night your soul will be required of you; then whose will those things be which you have provided?'

"So is he who lays up treasure for himself, and is not rich toward God" **(LUKE 12:16–21** NKJV**)**.

You Are Responsible for the Things You Own and the Things You Borrow

Whenever someone opens up a cistern or digs a new one and doesn't cover it and a bull or a donkey falls into it, the owner of the cistern must make up for the loss. He must pay money to the animal's owner, and then the dead animal will be his.

Whenever one person's bull kills another person's bull, they must sell the live bull and divide the money between them. They must divide the dead bull, too. However, if it was known that the bull had the habit of goring, and its owner didn't keep it confined, the owner must make up for the loss—bull for bull—and then the dead bull will be his."

The LORD continued, "Whenever someone steals a bull or a sheep and butchers it or sells it, he must make up for the loss with five head of cattle to replace the bull or four sheep to replace the sheep.

"If anyone catches a thief breaking in and hits him so that he dies, he is not guilty of murder. But if it happens after sunrise, he is guilty of murder.

"A thief must make up for what he has stolen. If he is unable to do so, he must be sold as a slave to pay for what he stole. But if the stolen animal is found alive in his possession, whether it's a bull, donkey, or a sheep, he must make up for the loss with double the amount.

"Whenever someone lets his livestock graze in a field or a vineyard, and they stray and graze in another person's field, he must make up for what the damaged field was expected to produce. But if he lets them ruin the whole field with their grazing, he must make up from his own field for the loss with the best from his field and vineyard.

"Whenever a fire starts and spreads into the underbrush so that it burns up stacked or standing grain or ruins a field, the person who started the fire must make up for the loss.

"This is what you must do whenever someone gives his neighbor silver or other valuables to keep for him, and they are stolen from that person's house: If the thief is caught, he must make up for the loss with double the amount. If the thief is not caught, the owner of the house must be brought to God to find out whether or not he took his neighbor's valuables. If there is a dispute over the ownership of a bull, a donkey, a sheep, an article of clothing, or any other lost property which two people claim as their own, both people must bring their case to God. The one whom God declares guilty must make up for his neighbor's loss with double the amount.

"This is what you must do whenever someone gives his neighbor a donkey, a bull, a sheep, or any other kind of animal to keep for him, and it dies, is injured, or is captured in war, and there are no witnesses. The case between them must be settled by swearing an oath to the Lord that the neighbor did not take the other person's animal. The owner must accept the oath. The neighbor doesn't have to make up for the loss. But if the animal was stolen from the neighbor, he must make up for the owner's loss. If it was killed by a wild animal, he must bring in the dead body as evidence. He doesn't have to make up for an animal that has been killed.

"Whenever someone borrows an animal from his neighbor, and it is injured or dies while the owner is not present, the borrower must make up for the loss" (**EXODUS 21:33–22:14** GOD'S WORD).

The law that God gave to the Israelites made sure that individuals respected other people's property and held individuals accountable for any harm that their property may have caused.

Using Wealth Poorly

The poor is disliked even by his neighbor, but the rich has many friends. **(PROVERBS 14:20 ESV)**

A rich man may have more friends than a poor man, but it's most likely his wealth that attracts them.

The name of the LORD is a strong tower; the righteous man runs into it and is safe. A rich man's wealth is his strong city, and like a high wall in his imagination. **(PROVERBS 18:10–11 ESV)**

Godly people trust the Lord, not their wealth.

Better to be poor and honest than to be dishonest and rich. **(PROVERBS 28:6 NLT)**

The rich man is wise in his own conceit; but the poor that hath understanding searcheth him out. **(PROVERBS 28:11 KJV)**

Then I looked again at vanity under the sun. There was a certain man without a dependent, having neither a son nor a brother, yet there was no end to all his labor. Indeed, his eyes were not satisfied with riches and he never asked, "And for whom am I laboring and depriving myself of pleasure?" This too is vanity and it is a grievous task. **(ECCLESIASTES 4:7–8 NASB)**

Sweet is the sleep of a laborer, whether he eats little or much, but the full stomach of the rich will not let him sleep. There is a grievous evil that I have seen under the sun: riches were kept by their owner to his hurt. **(ECCLESIASTES 5:12–13 ESV)**

Thus says the LORD: "Let not the wise man boast in his wisdom, let not the mighty man boast in his might, let not the rich man boast in his riches, but let him who boasts boast in this, that he understands and knows me, that I am the LORD who practices steadfast love, justice, and righteousness in the earth. For in these things I delight, declares the LORD" **(JEREMIAH 9:23–24 ESV)**.

Like a partridge that hatches eggs she has not laid, so are those who get their wealth by unjust means. At midlife they will lose their riches; in the end, they will become poor old fools. **(JEREMIAH 17:11 NLT)**

Yes, your wisdom has made you very rich, and your riches have made you very proud. **(EZEKIEL 28:5 NLT)**

This is God's message through the prophet Ezekiel to the king of Tyre.

But woe to you who are rich, for you are receiving your comfort in full. **(LUKE 6:24 NASB)**

Jesus gave this warning to rich people because they chose to gratify themselves now instead of focusing on spiritual things.

Promises of Abundance for God's People

This is what the LORD of Armies says: I am going to save my people from the land where the sun rises and from the land where the sun sets. I will bring them back, and they will live in Jerusalem. They will be my people, and I will be their God, who is faithful and just.

This is what the LORD of Armies says: Be strong so that the temple might be rebuilt, you people who are presently listening to the words from the mouths of the prophets who spoke when the foundation for the house of the LORD of Armies was laid.

Before that time there was no money to hire any person or animal. No one who traveled was safe from the enemy. I turned every person against his neighbor. But now I won't deal with the few remaining people as I did in earlier times, declares the LORD of Armies. Seeds will thrive in peacetime. Vines will produce their grapes. The land will yield its crops. The sky will produce its dew. I will give the few remaining people all these things as an inheritance. Just as you, people of Judah and people of Israel, have been a curse among the nations, so I will now save you, and you will become a blessing. Don't be afraid. Let your hands work hard.

This is what the LORD of Armies says: When your ancestors made me angry, I made plans to destroy you, declares the LORD of Armies, and I didn't change my plans. So now I have again made plans, but this time to do good to Jerusalem and the people of Judah. Don't be afraid. You must do these things: Speak the truth to each other. Give correct and fair verdicts for peace in your courts. Don't even think of doing evil to each other. Don't enjoy false testimony. I hate all these things, declares the LORD. **(ZECHARIAH 8:7–17 GOD'S WORD)**

These are encouraging words to Israel about future prosperity while they were in captivity.

———

Ho! Everyone who thirsts, come to the waters; and you who have no money, come, buy and eat. Yes, come, buy wine and milk without money and without price.

Why do you spend money for what is not bread, and your wages for what does not satisfy? Listen carefully to Me, and eat what is good, and let your soul delight itself in abundance. **(ISAIAH 55: 1–2 NKJV)**

———

I saw a new heaven and a new earth, because the first heaven and earth had disappeared, and the sea was gone. Then I saw the holy city, New Jerusalem, coming down from God out of heaven, dressed like a bride ready for her husband. I heard a loud voice from the throne say, "God lives with humans! God will make his home with them, and they will be his people. God himself will be with them and be their God. He will wipe every tear from their eyes. There won't be any more death. There won't be any grief, crying, or pain, because the first things have disappeared."

The one sitting on the throne said, "I am making everything new." He said, "Write this: 'These words are faithful and true.'" He said to me, "It has happened! I am the A and the Z, the beginning and the end. I will give a drink from the fountain filled with the water of life to anyone who is thirsty. It won't cost anything. Everyone who wins the victory will inherit these things. I will be their God, and they will be my children. But cowardly, unfaithful, and detestable people, murderers, sexual sinners, sorcerers, idolaters, and all liars will find themselves in the fiery lake of burning sulfur. This is the second death."

One of the seven angels who had the seven bowls full of the last seven plagues came to me and said, "Come! I will show you the bride, the wife of the lamb." He carried me by his power away to a large, high mountain. He showed me the holy city, Jerusalem, coming down from God out of heaven. It had the glory of God. Its light was like a valuable gem, like gray quartz, as clear as crystal. It had a large, high wall with 12 gates. Twelve angels were at the gates. The names of the 12 tribes of Israel were written on the gates. There were three gates on the east, three gates on the north, three gates on the south, and three gates on the west. The wall of the city had 12 foundations. The 12 names of the 12 apostles of the lamb were written on them.

The angel who was talking to me had a gold measuring stick to measure the city, its gates, and its wall. The city was square. It was as wide as it was long. He measured the city with the stick. It was 12,000 stadia long. Its length, width, and height were the same. He measured its wall. According to human measurement, which the angel was using, it was 144 cubits. Its wall was made of gray quartz. The city was made of pure gold, as clear as glass. The foundations of the city wall were beautifully decorated with all kinds of gems: The first foundation was gray quartz, the second sapphire, the third agate, the fourth emerald, the fifth onyx, the sixth red quartz, the seventh yellow quartz, the eighth beryl, the ninth topaz, the tenth green quartz, the eleventh jacinth, and the twelfth amethyst. The 12 gates were 12 pearls. Each gate was made of one pearl. The street of the city was made of pure gold, as clear as glass.

I did not see any temple in it, because the Lord God Almighty and the lamb are its temple. The city doesn't need any sun or moon to give it light because the glory of God gave it light. The lamb was its lamp. The nations will walk in its light, and the kings of the earth will bring their glory into it. Its gates will be open all day. They will never close because there won't be any night there. They will bring the glory and wealth of the nations into the holy city. Nothing unclean, no one who does anything detestable, and no liars will ever enter it. Only those whose names are written in the lamb's Book of Life will enter it. **(REVELATION 21:1–27 GOD'S WORD)**

Heaven will be a glorious place filled with wealth, wonder, and beauty. All our needs will be met and our joy will be full.

APPENDIX

THOUGHTS ON MONEY FROM JOHN WESLEY, GEORGE WHITEFIELD, AND C. H. SPURGEON

John Wesley (1703–1791), excerpt from his sermon "The Use of Money." Text from the 1872 edition— Thomas Jackson, editor

But let not any man imagine that he has done anything, barely by going thus far, by "gaining and saving all he can," if he were to stop here. All this is nothing, if a man go not forward, if he does not point all this at a farther end. Nor, indeed, can a man properly be said to save anything, if he only lays it up. You may as well throw your money into the sea, as bury it in the earth. And you may as well bury it in the earth, as in your chest, or in the Bank of England. Not to use, is effectually to throw it away. If, therefore, you would indeed "make yourselves friends of the mammon of unrighteousness," add the Third rule to the two preceding. Having, First, gained all you can, and, Secondly saved all you can, Then "give all you can."

In order to see the ground and reason of this, consider, when the Possessor of heaven and earth brought you into being, and placed you in this world, he placed you here not as a proprietor, but a steward: As such he entrusted you, for a season, with goods of various kinds; but the sole property of these still rests in him, nor can be alienated from him. As you yourself are not your own, but his, such is, likewise, all that you enjoy. Such is your soul and your body, not your own, but God's. And so is your substance in particular. And he has told you, in the most clear and express terms, how you are to employ it for him, in such a manner, that it may be all an holy sacrifice, acceptable through Christ Jesus. And this light, easy service, he has promised to reward with an eternal weight of glory.

The directions which God has given us, touching the use of our worldly substance, may be comprised in the following particulars. If you desire to be a faithful and a wise steward, out of that portion of your Lord's goods which he has for the present lodged in your hands, but with the right of resuming whenever it pleases him, First, provide things needful for yourself; food to eat, raiment to put on, whatever nature moderately requires for preserving the body in health and strength. Secondly, provide these for your wife, your children, your servants, or any others who pertain to your household. If when this is done there be an overplus left, then "do good to them that are of the household of faith." If there be an overplus still, "as you have opportunity, do good unto all men." In so doing, you give all you can; nay, in a sound sense, all you have: For all that is laid out in this manner is really given to God. You "render unto God the things that are God's," not only by what you give to the poor, but also by that which you expend in providing things needful for yourself and your household.

If, then, a doubt should at any time arise in your mind concerning what you are going to expend, either on yourself or any part of your family, you have an easy way to remove it. Calmly and seriously inquire, " (1.) In expending this, am I acting according to my character? Am I acting herein, not as a proprietor, but as a steward of my Lord's goods? (2.) Am I doing this in obedience to his Word? In what Scripture does he require me so to do? (3.) Can I offer up this action, this expense, as a sacrifice to God through Jesus Christ? (4.) Have I reason to believe that for this very work I shall have a reward at the resurrection of the just?" You will seldom need anything more to remove any doubt which arises on this head; but by this four-fold consideration you will receive clear light as to the way wherein you should go.

If any doubt still remain, you may farther examine yourself by prayer according to those heads of inquiry. Try whether you can say to the Searcher of hearts, your conscience not condemning you,

"Lord, thou seest I am going to expend this sum on that food, apparel, furniture. And thou knowest, I act herein with a single eye as a steward of thy goods, expending this portion of them thus in pursuance of the design thou hadst in entrusting me with them. Thou knowest I do this in obedience to the Lord, as thou commandest, and because thou commandest it. Let this, I beseech thee, be an holy sacrifice, acceptable through Jesus Christ! And give me a witness in myself that for this labour of love I shall have a recompense when thou rewardest every man according to his works." Now if your conscience bear you witness in the Holy Ghost that this prayer is well-pleasing to God, then have you no reason to doubt but that expense is right and good, and such as will never make you ashamed.

You see then what it is to "make yourselves friends of the mammon of unrighteousness," and by what means you may procure, "that when ye fail they may receive you into the everlasting habitations." You see the nature and extent of truly Christian prudence so far as it relates to the use of that great talent, money. Gain all you can, without hurting either yourself or your neighbour, in soul or body, by applying hereto with unintermitted diligence, and with all the understanding which God has given you;—save all you can, by cutting off every expense which serves only to indulge foolish desire; to gratify either the desire of flesh, the desire of the eye, or the pride of life; waste nothing, living or dying, on sin or folly, whether for yourself or your children;—and then, give all you can, or, in other words, give all you have to God.

George Whitefield (1714–1770), excerpt from sermon 47, "The Great Duty of Charity Recommended"

FIRST, I shall consider this duty, as relating to the bodies of men. And,

1. O that the rich would consider how praise-worthy this duty is, in helping their fellow-creatures! We were created to be a help to each other; God has made no one so independent as not to need the assistance of another; the richest and most powerful man upon the face of this earth, needs the help

and assistance of those who are around him; and though he may be great today, a thousand accidents may make him as low tomorrow; he that is rolling in plenty today, may be in as much scarcity tomorrow. If our rich men would be more charitable to their poor friends and neighbors, it would be a means of recommending them to the savor of others, if Providence should frown upon them; but alas, our great men had much rather spend their money in a playhouse, at a ball, an assembly, or a masquerade, than relieve a poor distressed servant of Jesus Christ. They had rather spend their estates on their hawks and hounds, on their whores, and earthly, sensual, devilish pleasures, than comfort, nourish, or relieve one of their distressed fellow-creatures. What difference is there between the king on the throne, and the beggar on the dunghill, when God demands their breaths? There is no difference, my brethren, in the grave, nor will there be any at the day of judgment. You will not be excused because you have had a great estate, a fine house, and lived in all the pleasures that earth could afford you; no, these things will be one means of your condemnation; neither will you be judged according to the largeness of your estate, but according to the use you have made of it.

Now, you may think nothing but of your pleasures and delights, of living in ease and plenty, and never consider how many thousands of your fellow-creatures would rejoice at what you are making waste of, and setting no account by. Let me beseech you, my rich brethren, to consider the poor of the world, and how commendable and praise-worthy it is to relieve those who are distressed. Consider, how pleasing this is to God, how delightful it is to man, and how many prayers you will have put up for your welfare, by those persons whom you relieve; and let this be a consideration

117

to spare a little out of the abundance wherewith God has blessed you, on the relief of his poor. He could have placed you in their low condition, and they in your high state; it is only his good pleasure that has thus made the difference, and shall not this make you remember your distressed fellow-creatures?

Let me beseech you to consider, which will stand you best at the day of judgment, so much money expended at a horse-race, or a cockpit, at a play or masquerade, or so much given for the relief of your fellow-creatures, and for the distressed members of Jesus Christ.

I beseech you, that you would consider how valuable and commendable this duty is: do not be angry at my thus exhorting you to that duty, which is so much recommended by Jesus Christ himself, and by all his apostles: I speak particularly to you, my rich brethren, to entreat you to consider those that are poor in this world, and help them from time to time, as their necessity calls for it. Consider, that there is a curse denounced against the riches of those, who do not thus do good with them; namely, "Go to now you rich men, weep and howl for your miseries that shall come upon you; your riches are corrupted, your garments are moth-eaten, your gold and silver is cankered, and the rust of them shall be a witness against you, and shall eat your flesh, as it were fire; ye have heaped your treasure together for the last day." You see the dreadful woe pronounced against all those who hoard up the abundance of the things of this life, without relieving the distresses of those who are in want thereof: and the apostle James goes on also to speak against those who have acquired estates by fraud, as too many have in these days. "Behold the hire of the laborers, which have reaped down your fields, which is by you kept back by fraud, crieth; and the cries of them who have reaped, are entered into the ears of the Lord God of Sabbaoth. Ye have lived in pleasure on the earth, and been wanton; ye have nourished your hearts, as in the day of slaughter." Thus, if you go on to live after the lust of the flesh, to pamper your bellies, and make them a god, while the poor all around you are starving, God will make these things a witness against you, which shall be as a worm to your souls, and gnaw your consciences to all eternity; therefore, let me once more recommend charity unto the bodies of men, and beseech you to remember what a blessed Lord Jesus Christ has promised unto those who thus love his members, that "as they have done it to the least of his members, they have done it unto him."

I am not now speaking for myself; I am not recommending my little flock in Georgia to you; then you might say, as many wantonly do, that I wanted the money for myself; no, my brethren, I am now recommending the poor of this land to you, your poor neighbors, poor friends, yea, your poor enemies; they are whom I am now speaking for; and when I see so many starving in the streets, and almost naked, my bowels are moved with pity and concern, to consider, that many in whose power it is, to lend their assisting hand, should shut up their bowels of compassion, and will not relieve their fellow-creatures, though in the most deplorable condition for the want thereof.

<hr />

As I have thus recommended charity particularly to the rich among you; so now I would,

2. SECONDLY, Recommend this to another set of people among us, who, instead of being the most forward in acts of charity, are commonly the most backward; I mean the clergy of this land.

119

Good God! How amazing is the consideration, that those, whom God has called out to labor in spiritual things, should be so backward in this duty, as fatal experience teacheth. Our clergy (that is the generality thereof) are only seeking after preferment, running up and down, to obtain one benefice after another; and to heap up an estate, either to spend on the pleasures of life, or to gratify their sensual appetites, while the poor of their flock are forgotten; nay, worse, they are scorned, hated, and disdained.

I am not now, my brethren, speaking of all the clergy; no, blessed be God, there are some among them, who abhor such proceedings, and are willing to relieve the necessitous; but God knows, these are but very few, while many take no thought of the poor among them.

They can visit the rich and the great, but the poor they cannot bear in their sight; they are forgetful, willfully forgetful of the poor members of Jesus Christ.

They have gone out of the old paths, and turned into a new polite way, but which is not warranted in the word of God: they are sunk into a fine way of acting; but as fine as it is, it was not the practice of the apostles, or of the Christians in any age of the church: for they visited and relieved the poor among them; but how rare is this among us, how seldom do we find charity in a clergyman?

It is with grief I speak these things, but woeful experience is a witness to the truth thereof: and if all the clergy of this land were here, I would tell them boldly, that they did not keep in the ways of charity, but were remiss in their duty; instead of "selling all and giving to the poor," they will not sell any thing, nor give at all to the poor.

3. THIRDLY, I would exhort you who are poor, to be charitable to one another.

Though you may not have money, or the things of this life, to bestow upon one another; yet you may assist them, by comforting, and advising them not to be discouraged though they are low in the world; or in sickness you may help them according as you have time or ability: do not be unkind to one another: do not grieve, or vex, or be angry with each other; for this is giving the world an advantage over you.

And if God stirs up any to relieve you, do not make an ill use of what his providence, by the hands of some Christian, hath bestowed upon you: be always humble and wait on God; do not murmur or repine, if you see any relieved and you are not; still wait on the Lord, and help one another, according to your abilities, from time to time.

C. H. Spurgeon (1834–1892), selections from *The Salt Cellars: Being a Collection of Proverbs, Together with Homely Notes Thereon*, Volume 2, M–Z 1889

Don't put all your eggs into one basket. It is unwise to risk all that you have in any one concern. If you have any savings, put them in several places. The marine form of this saying is: "Do not ship all your goods in one vessel."

Many can get money; few can use it well. Even to keep it is not easy. Many of the silliest investments have been made by men who, in their own business, were shrewd to the highest degree. It is harder to weave than to gather wool.

Many save their silver, but lose their souls. Many a man's soul has been ruined by his great love of money, although he had but little money to love.

Money borrowed is soon sorrowed. He that lends it begins to sorrow, even if the borrower does not; for, in general, he may mourn that he has parted from it to meet no more.

Money burns many. They are injured by their wealth. Some by bribes are burned; for when money's taken, freedom's forsaken.

Money calls, but does not stay; It is round and rolls away. It makes the mill to go, but it goes faster than the mill-wheel. It is no more to be kept in the purse than snow in an oven; at least, so I find it. But why should we wish it to stay? It is the circulating medium! Why should we detain it? If it rests it rusts. Let it go about doing good.

Money gained on Sabbath-day is a loss, I dare to say. No blessing can come with that which comes to us, on the devil's back, by our willful disobedience of God's law. The *loss of* health by neglect of rest, and the loss of soul by neglect of hearing the gospel, soon turn all seeming profit into real loss.

Money gilds over guilt. Money is said to be a composition for taking out stains in character; but, in that capacity, it is a failure. Those characters which can be thus gilded must surely be of the gingerbread order.

Money has no blood relations. There is no friendship in business. Sad that this should be a proverb in any land, but so it is. The Chinese *say:* "Though brothers are closely akin, it is each for himself in money matters." They also say: "Top and bottom teeth sometimes come into awkward collision." So little power has relationship in the savage customs of business that, in some instances, one hand would skin the other, if it could make a profit by it.

Money is a good servant, but a bad master. Even as a servant it is not easy to keep it in due subordination. If "money makes dogs dance," it makes men proud. If we make money our god, it will rule us like the devil.

Money speaks more powerfully than eloquence. Too often, because the speaker is a rich man he commands attention, and secures the approbation of persons who see no sound sense spoken by one who has no money bags. This is very well put in the following verse:—*The man of means is eloquent: Brave, handsome, noble, wise; All qualities with gold are, sent, And vanish where it flies.*

Money spent on the brain is never spent in vain. Pour your money into your brain, and you will never lose it all. Education is such a gain, that it is worth all that it costs, and more. Yet some fellows learn nothing in the schools. Many a father, when his son returns from the University, might say, "I put in gold into the furnace, and there came out this calf."

A hammer of gold will not open the gate of heaven. Money opens many of the gates of earth, for bribery is rife; but it has no power in the world to come. Money is more eloquent than ten members of parliament, but it cannot prevail with the Great Judge.

Better a purse empty than full of other men's money. Gaining riches by chicanery is drawing down a curse upon ourselves. Honorable poverty is infinitely to be preferred to dishonest wealth, or to large indebtedness. In the Telugu we read: "A cupful of rice-water without debt is enough."

Do good with your money, or it will do you no good. There is no power in it of itself to do real good to you. It may even do you evil; but, if used for God and his cause, and the poor, it will bless yourself.

NOTES

Chapter 7

1. *25 Billionaires and Millionaires That Became Philanthropists,* Business Pundit.com, August 4, 2008, www.businesspundit.com/25-billionaires-and-millionaires-that-became-philanthropists/

2. Girl Friday, the World's Richest Women: The Most Elite Women's Club, *Forbes* (blog), August 4, 2008, http://blogs.forbes.com/meghancasserly/2011/03/10/the-worlds-richest-women-billionaires

Chapter 9

3. Poverty Statistics and Poverty Causes. Poverty Statistics Central accessed April 30, 2011, http://povertystatistics.org/#axzz1JkRZqldc

4. Poverty in the United States Frequently Asked Questions. National Poverty Center accessed April 30, 2011, www.npc.umich.edu/poverty/#2